The Night Speaks

Also by Steven Forrest

The Inner Sky

The Changing Sky

The Book of Pluto

Measuring the Night
(with Jeffrey Wolf Green)

Measuring the Night Vol. 2
(with Jeffrey Wolf Green)

Stalking Anubis

Skymates (with Jodie Forrest)

Skymates II (with Jodie Forrest)

Yesterday's Sky

The Book of the Moon

The Book of Neptune

THE NIGHT SPEAKS

by Steven Forrest

Seven Paws Press, Inc.
Borrego Springs, CA

Published in 2016 by Seven Paws Press, Inc.
PO Box 82
Borrego Springs, CA 92004
www.sevenpaws.com

ISBN 978-1-939510-92-1

Cover photo by Aaron Dennis:
www.borregojeepphototours.com

Printed in the United States of America
LCCN 2016960533

TABLE OF CONTENTS

ACKNOWLEDGMENTS

To the lineage of astrologers, mostly unknown and forgotten, I owe nearly everything I know. For the rest, I thank those who over the years have allowed me to speak with them of their birthcharts and the lives they reflect. In body or out, you know who you are. Thank you.

In preparing this book, the assistance and insight of the following people have been particularly pivotal: Rob Lehmann, Chaquoia Mahaney, Al H. Morrison, Demetra George, Mary Ellen Glass, Jim Mullaney, Laura Frankstone, Bernie Ashman, Kathy Gartley, Antero Alli, Mikki Sligh, Bernard Rosenblum, Rick and Anji "Cakebread" Levine, Glenda Fletcher, Phyllis Smith-Hansen, Bill Janis, Chris Ford, and Alphee Lavoie.

And without the kindness, support, and patience of these people, nothing would have come to fruition: Dick and Bunny Forrest, Maritha Pottenger, Ed and Sylvia Kohus, Sara Romweber and Michael Rank, Poppy Z. Brite, Cynthia Wyatt, Mark Lerner, Gina Ceaglio, Maggie Nalbandian, Celeste Longacre, Linda Smith, Susan Dearborn Jackson, Carol Lavoie, Laura Glaser, Jean Michel Garcia and Catherine Losano, Camille Hildebrandt, Barbara Jensen, John Bien, Barbara Schermer, Deborah and Henry DaVega Wolfe, Rafi Nasser, Virginia Bell, Kate Wechsler, Carolyn and Richard Max, Gregory Jackson, Betty Pristera, Carol Czeczot, Sue and Tommy Field, Jeannie Rogers, Dick Mentock, Michel Ramos, Paul Hansen, Linda Belans, Ben Dyer, Melanie Jackson, Sinikka Laine and Cyril Beveridge, Michael Erlewine and the Matrix family, Eric Kurtz, Jo Hermann, Ruel Tyson, and the late Marty Bresnick, who once helped a curious twelve-year-old build his first astronomical telescope.

Ah, not to be cut off,
not through the slightest partition
shut out from the law of the stars.
The inner – what is it?
if not intensified sky,
hurled through with birds and deep
with the winds of homecoming.

—Rainer Maria Rilke

INTRODUCTION, 2016

Which one of your kids do you love the most? Anyone who actually answers that question obviously has no future in politics. In a similar way, authors, down the road in their careers, are often asked which of their books is their favorite. The stakes are lower, but the dilemma is the same. Books are like your kids.

Any book, at least any book worth writing, comes straight out of the marrow of your bones. If it gets a "good report card" from the critics, you glow—and you are tempted to show that review around like endless baby pictures. One bad review, and you metamorphose into mama bear facing down the bully who stole your kid's lunch box—even if the critics are right.

You love all your books, in other words, the warty ones no less than the handsome ones that go agreeably to bed at bedtime, make straight A's, and become class presidents.

But if you threaten me? If you say, Steve, confess! Which book is your favorite or you will face waterboarding, dentistry, and a tax audit, I would probably go with *The Night Speaks*. It was my fourth-born, but we've always had a special relationship. It brings me a lot of joy to bring this updated version to life. I am particularly happy that younger astrologers will now have it in their arsenal. As

I believe you will see, this is a different kind of astrology book, unlike any others you might have read. It is a book you might want to give to the people you love who think you are a little crazy because you believe in astrology.

Why might anyone have a favorite child, however secretly? I suspect the answer lies in some fundamental sympathy between their natures. Parent and child "understand each other," often wordlessly. One child got your eyes, another your nose. But sometimes there is one who seemed to get your soul. It has always been that way between me and *The Night Speaks.* These pages came whole-cloth straight out of my own DNA. Without a doubt, it is my most personal book. I am sure it reveals more about me than I know, or perhaps would even admit. Astrology has been a major focus of my spiritual experience. I have devoted my life to it. This is the book about why.

In 1984, Bantam Books published *The Inner Sky.* I was instantly catapulted from being an obscure young hippie in North Carolina to the lofty reaches of … well, astrological obscurity. But by the time my second book, *The Changing Sky*, came out in 1986, I was gaining some traction in the astrological world. In 1989 the third volume of my "Sky" trilogy, *Skymates,* was published. That one was coauthored with my then new wife, Jodie Forrest. By that time, I was a familiar face on the astrological speaking circuit.

I am still satisfied with those three volumes and happy that they remain available and widely-read after all these years. I often marvel at the fact that, had I everything to do over again, I would not change a word in any of them today in any substantive way.

My first three "children" have grown up and done well, in other words. I am proud of them. But fear not, I won't bore you with baby pictures.

My seven-year career with Bantam Books was a blessing, but it came to a natural ending. Bantam is a popular, mass-market publisher, while serious astrology is a niche market, not really in their marketing territory. The "Sky" trilogy sold well enough to be kept alive for longer than many paperbacks, but not well enough to be long-lived. It wasn't *Harry Potter* or the Holy Bible, in other words. One day, I got the news that all three books were all going out of print. In the language of the publishing industry, that meant that "the rights reverted to me." I could do what I wanted with the texts—not the physical books themselves as printed by Bantam. Those left unsold were destroyed. But the actual words I'd written: mine, all mine.

But what to do with them?

Angels intervened. The late, great Neil Michelsen had founded ACS Publications in 1973. He approached me about his company taking over all three "Sky" books. I was delighted—my babies would live to see their seventh birthdays! I only later found out that Neil was seriously ill at the time. He passed from this world in May 1990, shortly after we had signed the contract that kept my books—and my career—alive. I will always be grateful to him.

The Night Speaks was the first book I wrote specifically for ACS. They were hesitant when I proposed it, explaining that philosophical books "hadn't done well for them in the past." Understandably, the typical book-buying reader was looking for personal insight and encouragement in the vein of "self-help" books. But bless them, ACS, under the able guidance of Neil's widow, Maria K. Simms, and my editor there, Maritha Pottenger, agreed to go with my proposal. *The Night Speaks* was born. I had started the actual writing in 1988 or so. It was finally published in 1993—writing a book takes a while, but even after the author types "The End," a lot of wheels have to turn before a reader holds the printed volume in his or her hands. I was already well into writing *The Book of Pluto* by the time *The Night Speaks* came off the conveyer belt.

Meanwhile I had turned forty years old. Under the unsettling rays of my Uranian Opposition, I felt the need to break out of some fixed patterns in my life, to do something a bit more radical. My books were doing well. I was lecturing around the country. My private astrological practice was getting bigger all the time. I had some famous clients. I'd "hung out with rock stars."

But I still felt like being an astrologer was like living in a ghetto.

In the original Foreword to *The Night Speaks*, I wrote, "Since the 1960s, in both North America and Europe, an astrological renaissance has occurred … I've watched it unfold … Over and over again, I've been struck by one overwhelming and dispiriting observation: hardly anyone outside the narrow walls of the astrological community or its committed clients even knows that the renaissance has taken place. To the person on the street, it might as well not have happened."

That was the dilemma I wanted to address in *The Night Speaks*.

I loved astrology passionately. Every day I saw it helping people. But in the street, astrology was still mostly viewed as silliness. Anyone who "believed in it" was taken for a fool. Could I write the book an open-minded critic might read and perhaps be moved to give astrology an hour's chance to prove itself? Could I write a book that my clients could confidently hand their skeptical friends? Could I break through the monumental wall of prejudice and ignorance that kept astrology trapped in its ghetto?

I had written three "How To" books.

It was time to write a "Why To."

For better or worse, we live in an age in which scientific evidence is often taken to be the final truth of any matter. I knew that any convincing work about "why to" use astrology would have to address the rational reasons for entertaining the idea that it might actually work. There are many! You will encounter a great number of them in the pages that follow.

As early as chapter two, I dive into what to me is probably the single most compelling and obvious piece of objective evidence for a connection between the sky and human affairs: the sunspot cycle. Most astrologers are unaware of it. As you will see, they should not be. Even though sunspots are a far cry from "Gemini" and "Libra," I know of no single area where astrology—in the larger sense of the word—can prove itself so decisively, simply, and quickly to anyone who knows even the rudiments of recent history.

In terms of pursuing an argument for astrology that passes the "science test," there is another reason to be excited about sunspots: they come with very little baggage. A person who reflexively bristles at the word "astrology" might very well listen curiously if we say, "There was once this Russian scientist who was sent to the Gulag because he had found evidence that sunspots, rather than class struggle, had driven history ..."

Bless the scientists. Bless the noble human aspiration to learn the objective truth of how the universe works. But, to me, it is perilous for astrologers to feel that if we want to be taken seriously, we must become little scientists. We can pass that science test, but we can do so much more than that. We are the priesthood of the sacred sky—creatures of the Moon as much as of the Sun. There are compelling, poetic, heart-centered arguments for astrology. In writing *The Night Speaks*, I wanted to be very careful to hold that banner high and unabashedly. I did not want to bow before those pre-Quantum scientists who still believe in the myth of the separate, objective observer. I am happy to bring my team to play on their home court, but I don't want to forget that I have a home court of my own.

You will see that approach right from the outset of chapter one, which is an account of the simple heart-impact of the night sky from the deck of a sloop out ghosting on dark waters under the stars.

In bringing *The Night Speaks* back into print after a long and complicated hiatus, I considered rewriting it in a major way but decided against doing that—with a few significant exceptions. In many respects, this is the book almost exactly as it was published in 1993. I've put a little literary polish on it here and there. Joltingly archaic references have been updated—many of my younger readers would not, for example, know what a "VCR" was, so it has morphed into "a video screen."

Apart from those tweaks, there are two major additions to the original text.

First, my analysis of the correlations between human events and the sunspot cycle had ended in 1990. I've added a lengthy section which follows that cycle up to the present moment. The reasons are obvious—but I also really wanted my younger readers to see these energies operating in the shapes of the times they had actually experienced directly themselves.

Second, in the original volume, there was a section called "The Year 2000." I've retained the heart of that writing, which was an analysis of the epochal Uranus-Neptune of the early 1990s—but I deleted the rest. What is gone was a look at a set of relatively trivial transits leading up to the turn of the millennium. At this point in time, all that material felt like yesterday's news. I knew that if I as the author was bored reading it ... well, pity you, the poor innocent reader. I replaced those deleted pages with a detailed, reflective look backwards at the Uranus-Neptune conjunction from the perspective of today.

Essentially, that rather rare planetary alignment predicted a major change in the mythology and assumptions upon which whole societies rest. When I wrote those pages originally, the conjunction itself was still in the future. I could only gaze into the crystal ball of astrological symbolism. Now in 2016, while it is important to remember that the cycle still has a century and half to play out, we can begin to see some of the handwriting on the wall—and to evaluate the prophetic accuracy of our crystal ball.

You can judge that prophetic accuracy yourself. My original words are all still here, unchanged.

Science has marched on over the past quarter-century. Most pressingly for astrological purposes, right as *The Night Speaks* was published in 1992, the first of the "trans-Neptunian" worlds was discovered orbiting out beyond Pluto. It was small and it easily passed under the collective radar. But the discovery of much-larger Eris in 2005 hit the cover of *TIME* magazine as "The Tenth Planet." Shortly thereafter, both Eris and Pluto were demoted to "dwarf planets," while a thousand more little worlds were found out there in the solar system's deep freeze.

There's a Uranus-Neptune paradigm shift for you! Astrology is reeling—or should be—as we internalize this major extension of the text we are all reading: the sky itself.

None of that material got into *The Night Speaks*. I simply didn't know about it. No one did. If you are interested, I've covered it in some detail in my most recent work, *The Book of Neptune*, which was published in early 2016.

The scientific investigation of astrology and biophysical areas relevant to it has marched on too. The simple truth is that I am not in that parade any more. Life is short and we all need to make difficult choices about our priorities. My focus for the past three decades has been on what one might call "the clinical application" of astrological work—helping people one at a time as best I can, along with assisting others in learning how to do that good work themselves via my various teaching programs. With that mission to occupy me, I've got a perpetual tiger by the tail. There is little time left over for anything else. Bottom line, I have not stayed current with the work of my more scientifically-oriented colleagues.

Rather than stepping onto the perilously thin ice of my own ignorance, I decided not to update those parts of *The Night Speaks*. All the science in the book is pre-1990. If you are drawn to learn about the current state of that kind of material, let me refer you to the work of David

Cochrane. He's the past president of the International Society for Astrological Research, and is a fine source of contemporary information on this aspect of the field. Here's a link to get you started: www.astrosoftware.com/AstrologyArticle.htm

My old friend Alphee Lavoie has been very active in doing statistical astrological research as well. Here's a link to his group of astrological investigators—known to the world as *the 'gators*: www.astroinvestigators.com

Change is eternal, and a bumpy road sometimes. My marriage to Jodie Forrest, to whom there are many references in this book, dissolved after exactly one complete Saturn cycle. These pages are a time capsule; she is still my wife in them.

Again in keeping with my intention of letting *The Night Speaks* be something of a time capsule, I've retained the original Acknowledgments page. Some people mentioned there have left this world, while many have left my life in one way or another. The wheels turn. The book would not have existed without them, so I here again honor and thank them.

To that list I would add my faithful and hyper-competent manager, friend, and cyber-wizard, Tony Howard. Very little that I do would be possible without him. I also thank our dedicated copy editor Carol Czeczot. And finally, my gratitude to Michelle Kondos for filling our home with paintings and my heart with light.

—Steven Forrest
Borrego Springs, California
July 2016

FOREWORD
HOW I GOT MY JOB

Indulge me for a few seconds …

People fly from far away to see me. My waiting list is a year long. Some of my clients have names you'd recognize. Earnest strangers walk up to me in restaurants and say, "Aren't you … ?" I've been on TV. I've been on the radio. I've been interviewed more times than I can remember. I fly all over the country and speak to large audiences. I have three books about my work in print, translated into several languages. *Esquire* called one of them "truly outstanding." A line from the first book appeared—honor of honors—as the answer to a Sunday *New York Times* acrostic puzzle.

All that ego-adrenaline, and yet I live with a primal fear: it's the thought that somebody's conservative grandfather will come up to me at a party and ask that simple, ubiquitous social question, "By the way, Steve, what do you do?"

Often I say "counselor," and try artfully to squirm away from the subject. Occasionally, and never among the Gifted and Talented, I've assumed an intimidatingly professorial air and intoned, "Psychological Astronomer."

But inevitably there are times when artifice fails and the truth comes out: I am an astrologer.

Perhaps it's the reflectiveness that comes with turning forty. Perhaps it is a response to the "spokesperson" role I play from time to time. But lately I find myself thinking dark and complicated thoughts about science and history, cosmos and consciousness, truth and lies … all pivoting around one humbling self-observation: I'm sometimes embarrassed to say what I do. I'm embarrassed to say I'm an astrologer.

It shouldn't be that way, I know. One reason is that I simply have a lot of respect for my clients. In any other area I would honor their collective judgments. By and large, the men and women whom I counsel are bright, educated, dynamic individuals, the people who shape the life of my community. They're psychotherapists and physicians, architects, professors, novelists, lawyers and artists of every discipline. They're ministers, executives, stockbrokers, true leaders in the hardheaded world of business … miles away from the "hapless victims of astrological charlatans" so often lamented in the anti-astrology press. And they return to me year after year. They encourage their friends to make appointments with me. With their support, I prosper.

And of course, I wouldn't have their support if I didn't give them something they value.

I value it too, despite my embarrassment. Astrology, when approached seriously, provides personal, concrete, "feel-able" proof that we inhabit a meaningful universe. Properly applied and understood, it restores to the cosmos some of the mystery and enchantment that modern life tends to sap, and it accomplishes that without asking us to surrender our intellects. Carl Jung, the seminal psychoanalyst, called astrology the repository of all the psychological knowledge of ancient humanity. The modem bard Robert Bly describes it as "the great intellectual triumph of the Mother civilization."

But those voices are in the minority. Most educated people today have been programmed to put astrology in the same benighted category as human sacrifice.

Who's to blame? First on the list are astrologers themselves, at least some of us. The majesty, emotional valence, and intellectual rigor of the astrological symbolism has often been reduced to cutesy Sun Sign formulas. "A Libran male can be as cranky as a crocodile with poison ivy, and his habit of rationalizing everything, including love, will drive you to a frenzy ..." (Linda Goodman; *Sun Signs*). "Rotters and eyelash-batters are found in this sign, it's true. Libras aren't usually afraid to mooch or wrangle some way of getting themselves taken care of ..." (Debbi Kempton-Smith; *Secrets from a Stargazer's Notebook*).

Mohandas Gandhi was a Libran. So was Eleanor Roosevelt.

Who can take silly one-liners such as those seriously? Not me. Not anyone with enough brains to brush his or her teeth without injury.

"Well, Steve, what do you do for a living?" When I hear that question, 1 know I'm trapped. I can lie. Or I can tell the truth—and know that what will be heard is a lie.

I am not alone in this predicament. According to *TIME* magazine of May 16, 1988, some fifty million Americans believe in astrology, an attitude which *TIME* characterizes as a "charming eccentricity." Count on it: every one of those people has at least a couple of friends who are convinced that their use of astrology is evidence that they're soft in the head.

Astrology was not always so ridiculed. Pythagoras believed in astrology. So did Galileo and Plato. Johannes Kepler, too. And Hippocrates, the "Father of Medicine." Throughout the lion's share of human history, in virtually every society, the validity of some form of astrology was taken to be self-evident.

Of course, so were the ideas that the earth was flat and that God had a long white beard.

But astrology is different. Its claims are demonstrable and testable, at least subjectively. Isaac Newton's servant once said of his master, "I never knew him to take any recreation or pastime either in riding out to take the air, walking, bowling, or any other exercise whatever, thinking all hours lost that were not spent in his studies …"

Isaac Newton was a Capricorn, a sign that emphasizes self-discipline and seriousness of purpose. While his attitude toward astrology is not known definitively, it is clear that he was immersed in the metaphysical and alchemical perspectives of his era—perspectives intimately interwoven with the astrological worldview. Had Newton read that his nature was playful and sociable, would he have believed it? Would he have not been moved to comment negatively?

God's beard is tough to study. Human nature isn't. We see it everywhere. And Newton, arguably the most acute observer who ever lived, never felt moved to criticize astrology, even though it is a virtual certainty he had contact with it.

What happened? How did astrology lose its credibility? Why is there a dusty little shelf in the back corner of every bookstore labeled "Astrology, Occult, UFOs"? The story is long and winding. I'll tell some of it in the pages that follow. But here it is in a single line: the *National Enquirer* got its hands on the symbolism. That's not history exactly, but it captures the essence of the catastrophe. Far more deeply, astrology's current predicament is linked to a clash of paradigms—those all-embracing sets of assumptions which shape the way a culture looks at life. In astrology, the universe is purposeful and alive, and we are in communion with it. This notion, so attractive at first glance, is actually quite subversive. It challenges the domination of our minds and spirits by the mechanistic, disenchanted view of human existence that has us all staring at video screens, waiting for the world to end.

Since the 1960s, in both North America and Europe, an astrological renaissance has occurred. Many factors have spurred it: the widespread return to the "old religion" celebrating the sacredness of earth, sky and consciousness itself; the popularization of psychotherapy as a developmental avenue for "normal" people; the advent of microcomputers which have made astrology's formidable mathematics less of a barrier; the success of small, specialized publishing enterprises, which have in three decades produced a body of technical astrological literature unrivaled in history.

I've watched it unfold. I know a lot of the personalities involved. Many of them I would call friends. In a small way, I've been part of the process. Over and over again, I've been struck by one overwhelming and dispiriting observation: hardly anyone outside the narrow walls of the astrological community or its committed clients even knows that the renaissance has taken place. To the person on the street, it might as well not have happened.

Why?

The answer, I think, is tied up with my embarrassment ...

Astrology has a terrible public relations problem. To that person on the street, it still looks dumb. Or irrelevant. Or like something "he could safely laugh at," as Jung put it.

The book you hold in your hands is no "coffee table" giggle about Sun Signs, nor is it a technical how-to manual such as my *Sky* trilogy. Instead, it is an extended essay on modern astrology: what it is, what it isn't, and how it might enhance your life. Unlike my previous books, this one is very personal, and I make no effort to conceal that. Astrology has been the professional, and in many ways the spiritual, focus of my life. I want to share the reasons why, and some of those reasons are inseparable from my own subjective experiences.

I'll tell the truth as I see it, with one exception. To protect the privacy of my clients and the security of some of my non-astrological sources, I'll sometimes distort certain biographical or circumstantial facts not relevant to the points I'm elucidating.

My intention is to produce a book an intelligent "believer" could offer his or her skeptical friends. I want to demonstrate, as best I can, that astrology is intellectually plausible and spiritually healthy today, much as it was in Neolithic villages, among the gleaming pyramids, in Renaissance chambers where Leonardo walked ...

Here, in a nutshell, is the book I pray that conservative grandfather might have read before he buttonholes me at the party and says, "Steve, tell me, what do you do for a living?"

—Steven Forrest
Chapel Hill, North Carolina
Summer Solstice, 1991

To the Memory of
Michel Gauquelin

PART ONE

THE BOUNDLESS
SYMBOL

1

NIGHT

Such a strange feeling … sort of like dying, if all the hopeful things we say about dying are true …

We'd arrived late at the salt-creek where my old wooden trimaran, *Nimble Hope*, lay tied to her berth. Three of us had made the tiring drive from Chapel Hill. Normally, we'd sleep on board, then set sail for the weekend's adventures on Saturday morning. But tonight, the stars called. We cast off—and soon entered a realm we modern people too easily forget.

The estuary of the Neuse River is wide off the village of Oriental, almost an inland sea. In an hour, the lights of either shore were a sparse string of pearls, barely defining a fairy horizon between the pulsing blackness of the night and the deeper blackness of the waters. We hung suspended, coasting between two infinite Nights, one full of stars, the other full of finny creatures.

The wind was light but held steady; the battered sails of the big trimaran pulled us as though they were gentle, invisible hands. Only the gurgle of black water under wooden hulls broke the silence.

Occasionally, the beaches of the Carolina coast are blessed with a bloom of phosphorescent plankton. Waves break and recede, leaving glittering stars among the litter of shells. Tonight was such a time, but we were miles from any sea-strand, out in the open reaches of the Neuse. The plankton remained dark, except where our three hulls disturbed them. Then they exploded into eerie galaxies, trailing out behind us like elfin highways.

An hour passed. Jane turned in below, leaving Michele and me to stare into the darkness. Overhead, the Milky Way radiated supernal light. A billion suns, incomprehensibly distant, melded into a dim veil, as though some ghostly bride lurked just beyond the southern horizon. In my hand, the helm quivered now and then, reminding me that the night wind still animated our starship.

Off the bows, in the midst of the sunless waters, a tiny cloud of gray light appeared. Then another, and another. Sea nettles—a kind of jellyfish—are always common in these bays and river mouths. Normally they're invisible after dark. Not now. They'd been feasting on plankton, as usual. But tonight that plankton glowed, and so did the near-transparent sea nettles.

The Milky Way was blown glass. The luminous sea nettles made it look like shards of it had plunged to earth, shattering, scattering ghost-fragments of gray luminosity across the invisible waves.

The wind died. The black water became a mirror facing the night sky. Among the glowing jellyfish there now gleamed pinpricks of light. Vega. Altair. Deneb. Albiero. Markab. Caph. Alpheratz—the stars of summer, reflected in the syrupy, slow water. We drifted silently, with blackness above us, blackness below, and everything radiant with stars and ghosts, everything pregnant, everything becoming, becoming, becoming ...

Midnight came and went. Still we floated, becalmed, breathless, afraid even to whisper. Suddenly a blaze of brilliant light shocked the zenith, sundering bright Cassiopeia, disappearing somewhere in Cepheus, the faint king: a meteor. A falling star. One of the last messengers of the Perseid shower. As the night wore on, dozens more shooting stars ignited the upper atmosphere. Our sky blazed with invaders, mirrored in the motionless black water. They darted among stars and radiant jellyfish, punctuating a message no mind could decipher.

Where were we?

Embarked in our fragile vessel, sailing the waters of a dangerous, mysterious universe ... *what were we?* Consciousness. Bodies. But were we not cells in some greater body? Were we not somehow made of the same stuff as the glowing star-clouds, the falling Perseids, the phosphorescent bodies of the sea nettles? Were we not all locked in some unknowable harmony?

As *Nimble Hope* floated through that memorable night, our spirits brimmed with reverence, awe, even a spice of fear. But above all, bliss: what bliss to be an intelligence alive to this heartbreakingly perfect cosmos.

And what did the universe itself feel? Was it insensible to its own vibrant life? Certainly such doubts never crossed our minds that night. With our critical functions stunned into humility and silence by the weight of the sky's presence, with our educations and presumptions left on the distant shore, we beheld the night as did our Paleolithic foremothers and forefathers.

We beheld the night as a living creature.

The sky is alive. How strange those words sound. How primitive. How far from the myths they spin for us in schools. But try the alternative: the sky is dead. We inhabit a dead universe.

So where's the truth? Is the cosmos alive or inanimate? Do we live inside a vast thought or inside a vast clock?

Trust your senses. Engage your heart. Few of us have been so impoverished by the "riches" of our industrial civilization that we've never seen the night as I saw it from the deck of *Nimble Hope*. Tune into your memory banks. Remember the stars arching over your head somewhere long ago. Recall the thrill of recognition that surged through you. The thrill of life meeting life.

That is the soul of astrology.

Schools of thought come and go, crashing and breaking like waves on the opaque shores of reality. The Babylonians had eighteen Signs for a while; we have twelve. Passionate debates rage about how to calculate the houses of the horoscope. Most Western astrologers begin their zodiac with the Sun's position on the first day of spring; most Eastern ones start with the Sun's entry into the constellation Aries. Astrology today is a disorderly system, without much internal agreement ... we sound as bad as physicists discussing gravity or economists explaining the latest downturn.

No matter. Each school of thought, each astrological theory, is an attempt to do the impossible: to unravel the great symbol of the living sky. Not "to give it meaning." Palpably, the sky already has meaning; just look up and feel it. Astrology's task is to put that overwhelming emotion into words. To take that vast thought, always just beyond our reach, and turn it into something comprehensible.

We can't do it. But we can try, and the trying reflects a yearning deep in every one of us … a yearning to feel the same heart beating inside us that beats inside star-clouds and sea nettles.

The wind stirred *Nimble Hope*'s mainsail and Michele and I stirred from our meditations. Slowly, our little vessel began to cut through the dark water. Jane still snoozed in her berth, and the Milky Way still glowed overhead, but more dimly now; a faint light loomed in the east. Soon the sun would rise, washing out plankton and stars.

Bleary-eyed, we steered our aged trimaran toward the welcoming blink of a lighted buoy a mile or two distant. We dared not start the noisy Evinrude outboard motor. It would have been like singing "Hang on Sloopy" in a cathedral. Eventually, *Nimble Hope* ghosted into an anchorage in nearby Adams Creek. We dropped the hook as the last star faded into blue. Soon we were asleep.

But the heavens never sleep. In the heart of Scorpio, at the limits of human visibility, a faint light moved. Starlike, it was the planet Uranus, harbinger of upheaval. Taking eighty-four years to make a single circuit of the sun, it resonates in the human world with the process of *individuation*—the process whereby we "molt," often traumatically, all that is inauthentic in our lives. Metaphorically, its action is often likened to that of a lightning bolt.

When I took my first breath of air in this world, the waning degrees of Scorpio were rising in the east. Thus, my "Ascendant" is Scorpio, and I will forever be sensitive to astrological events occurring there.

Seeing Uranus approaching that hot-wired part of my birthchart, a fortune-teller would have pronounced, "Expect the unexpected."

A pessimist would have warned, "Pain and trouble."

An optimist, closer to my blood, would have prophesied, "Opportunity, but you'll have to seize it."

To a client, nowadays, I might say, "Time to crack out of your egg, little chicken. Too long you've been doing what's expected of you, pleasing your Sunday school teachers. You're in this living universe for a purpose. It's time to figure out what that purpose is and do something about it. And, by the way, Cosmic Intelligence is going to pitch in and help you out …"

Uh oh.

Within a year, *Nimble Hope*'s mast came crashing down in an accident that would have made good movie footage. I came as close to getting killed as I ever have. Nothing so sets the mind upon Questions Eternal.

Shortly thereafter Michele and I parted.

And out of the blue, I got a contract with a major publisher to write what would prove to be my first book, *The Inner Sky*.

Before the dust settled a year or two later, I had met Jodie, the woman who would become my second wife.

"Uranus transiting the Ascendant." That was the astrological correlate for what, in human terms, was the most momentous year of my life. And it's just one of a practically limitless number of ways in which consciousness and cosmos interact.

Reader, you and I are both sailing the same mysterious waters. We're born, and from that moment we carry inside ourselves a little hologram of the sky. As long as we live, it resonates with the rhythms of planets and tides, stars and seasons. That hologram is our life. Its breath is the breathing of an intelligent, conscious universe.

Studying that hologram is the delicate, ever-changing art we call astrology.

2

SUN

Poetically, astrology makes sense. The luminous depths of the sky stand as a metaphor for other, more subjective depths: those of consciousness itself. But there's a long leap from that idea to the notion that "being an Aries" means anything. In fact, to modern sensibilities, the claim that our natures and destinies are reflected in the sky seems like lunacy, right up there with, "I met Elvis on a UFO."

Cards on the table: I want to convince your logical brain that astrology merits your open-minded consideration. I make no apologies for appealing to your heart, to your aesthetic sensibilities, and to your appreciation of the numinous. I did so in recounting my adventure aboard *Nimble Hope*, and I'll do so many times again in the pages that follow. It is, in my opinion, arrogant to imply that all that cannot be measured and quantified is unreal. Too much of what it means to be human is sacrificed on that altar.

But I also want to speak to your intellect, and to your rational hesitations. Poetry is fine, but what about common sense? In the real world, among real people, does astrology actually work?

Obviously, I think so. I also believe that if you stick with me for a few more pages, you'll be at least halfway convinced yourself. There is an astrological rhythm so powerful, so obvious, so easily demonstrated, that its efficacy can hardly be denied.

THE SUNSPOT CONNECTION

Remember the frantic intensity of the late sixties? New heroes and mythologies sprang out of nowhere. Naïve confidence ran rampant. Vietnam provided a crucifixion story and an evocative emotional rallying point. Bob Dylan, the Beatles and a generation of singer-songwriters orchestrated the drama with rousing anthems and irresistible manifestos. The advent of the Pill spiced the stew with the scent of sex. Think what you will about the foolish excesses and runaway herd instinct of those years, they were exciting times. But did history excite us, or did we excite history? Was humanity simply ready to stir up the *zeitgeist*? It's the proverbial question of the chicken and the egg.

Meanwhile, ninety-three million miles away, gargantuan nuclear storms swirled across the troubled face of the sun. Great solar prominences exploded in hundred-thousand-mile high cascades of fire. Blasts of charged particles and waves of magnetism roared away from the sun, engulfing the Earth and planets. The eleven-year cycle of solar storms had reached its crescendo. For our central star, the late sixties marked the season of fire – sunspot maximum.

Whatever engines drove that wild chapter of our national history, they certainly had run out of gas by the middle 1970s. Remember the disco wasteland? Gerald Ford? The "me" generation? Remember the confusion and floundering of our national leadership in the aftermath of Watergate and the OPEC-engineered energy crisis?

We might be annoyed by the naïveté and blind enthusiasm of the late sixties, but no one who lived through them would be likely to call them boring. And no matter how charitable a view we take of the middle seventies, by most standards the "energy crisis" of those years was not limited to oil fields and gas pumps.

Throughout the middle 1970s, the face of the sun was tranquil. Gone were the great magnetic storms of the late sixties. The season of calm—the sunspot minimum—had arrived.

Is this astrology? Certainly not in a traditional sense. Sunspots have nothing to do with Leo or Sagittarius. Nonetheless, whenever w notice a correlation between cosmic events and human affairs, we've entered the astrological realm.

Aleksandr Leonidovich Chizhevsky – a biologist, not an astrologer – was the first to notice the pattern: the intensity of human events peaks during sunspot maximum and slacks off at the minimum. He was a Soviet researcher, brilliant, but badly placed in history. Marxist theory prefers class struggles to solar storms as the drivers of history. Chizhevsky learned that lesson the hard way, spending twenty years exiled in the Gulag as punishment for his research. He died in 1964.

Subsequently, the Soviets have recognized the validity of his observations. In early 1968, the Moscow Society of Naturalists held a posthumous meeting in his honor. Sunspots – and Chizhevsky – were rehabilitated.

Sunspots occur cyclically in a variable period with an *average* length of about 11.1 years. In this, they are unlike other astrological cycles which normally can be predicted with near-perfect accuracy. Despite the sunspot cycle being somewhat elastic, Chizhevsky stated his theories with great precision. He divided the solar cycle into four distinct phases, each associated with a particular set of human attitudes and motivations. He claimed that the rhythm of sunspots correlated with all major mass movements—wars, migrations, religious revivals—since the fifth century BC.

Here is a brief overview of Chizhevsky's outline:

- *Phase One:* **The solar minimum.** With sunspot activity at its eleven-year low, humanity is in an easygoing mood, tolerant but lazy. People are occupied with personal concerns and little inclined to organize themselves into any kind of unified, history-shaping force.

- *Phase Two:* **The solar increase.** Social energies begin to coalesce. Exciting new ideas and charismatic spokespeople appear, planting seeds that quickly germinate into mass movements. Alliances form. According to Chizhevsky, at this point in the cycle some fundamental problem arises and demands radical solution.

- *Phase Three:* **The solar maximum.** Energies abound. Everyone is excited, eager to respond *en masse* to leadership or inspiration, for better or worse. An air of enthusiastic drunkenness suffuses the polity. Emigration increases. Wars begin. Tension is high.

- *Phase Four:* **The solar decline.** Exhausted and often disenchanted, humanity now loses steam. The seductive easy answers of the previous several years break down. Unity and collective focus drop off. Disillusionment increases. Groups disband. People go back to tending their own gardens— and gradually we descend again into the peaceful lassitude of Phase One, the sunspot minimum.

Chizhevsky divided the four solar phases into periods of three, two, three and three years respectively. Due to the varying lengths of the cycle, it is best to take those numbers as ratios. Once, two maxima were observed only seven years apart. Another time, seventeen years elapsed between maxima. For unknown reasons, hardly any sunspots were observed between 1645 and 1715—years which, incidentally, were among the most peaceful in human history.

Now for the $64,000 question: how accurate is Chizhevsky's theory? Does the sunspot cycle really have any bearing on terrestrial experience, or is that idea just hocus-pocus dressed up in a few anecdotes and lucky coincidences? Finding an answer that holds up to rigorous scrutiny is not easy. Chizhevsky himself tried to quantify his hypotheses in a testable form. He drew up a chart which he claimed showed all major wars and social uprisings for the last two millennia. Analyzing these events in the light of his four solar phases, he concluded that almost 80% of them occurred during Phases Two and Three – the solar increase and the maximum. Only five percent occurred during the quiescent period of Phase One.

Chizhevsky's work can be faulted on two counts. First, there is the obvious problem of deciding what exactly constitutes a "major" uprising or social change. There is inevitably a subjective component to such judgments, and a list assembled by a disinterested third party would be more convincing, if the pattern still held.

The second objection to Chizhevsky's methodology is more serious. It has to do with the accuracy of his sunspot data. The Chinese observed sunspots as early as 28 BC. The sun-worshipping Inca knew that their sun-god, Inti, "had blemishes on his face." But regular solar observation dates back only to Galileo, in the early seventeenth century. Even then, it was crude and irregular. Since the sunspot cycle itself is somewhat irregular, Chizhevsky's historical correlations become suspect before Galileo, and shaky for a century or so after him.

Chizhevsky's approach was to extrapolate the eleven-year cycle backwards, interpolating between the scattered smattering of sunspot data that have come down from pre-Renaissance sources. Obviously, that's a questionable method.

Was Chizhevsky wrong, then? Happily, you can judge that for yourself. Unlike more abstruse astrological questions, the sunspot connection can be researched with equipment no more elaborate than an encyclopedia. Look at the following graph. It plots the annual mean sunspot number since 1730, which is around the time the observations become consistent and reliable enough to not leave us doubting.

With one glance at the graph, immediately the pronounced cyclical quality of the solar storms is evident. Equally evident is the great variability of the cycle. Some peaks are vastly stormier than others. Some lows are only relative, while others truly represent "the year of the quiet sun." Furthermore, the pattern seems distorted by unknown and apparently random factors, leading to multiple peaks and out-of-season "spikes."

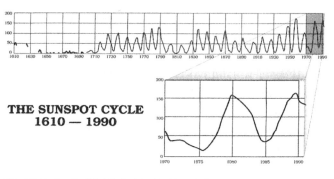

**THE SUNSPOT CYCLE
1610 — 1990**

1610 – 1970, taken from John Gribbin's *The Death of the Sun*, Delacorte, 1980.
1970 – 1990, plotted by author.

The year 1775 shows a rather deep minimum followed by a meteoric two-year climb to one of the most fiery peaks in the history of solar observation. The American Revolution, of course, ignited during this period. New leaders arose and their new ideas fell on receptive ears. In this case, at least, the facts are strikingly consistent with Chizhevsky's theories.

The next solar minimum occurred around 1783—and in September of that year, in Paris, the Treaty of

Peace with Britain was signed. Fighting had actually ended about two years earlier, as we swung down toward the minimum in Phase Three.

The late 1780s saw another solar peak, and once again the flames of unrest were fanned. The Bastille was stormed and the French Revolution exploded.

The subsequent ascending solar cycle, culminating in a rather low peak, marked the rise of Napoleon, who was declared Emperor of the French in 1805 after a series of military and political victories.

The year 1830 saw another peak in sunspot activity and another revolution in France. Once again, masses of men and women took to the streets, and again, a French king was deposed. That pattern was destined to be repeated a third time in the bloody French street rioting of 1848 that led to the establishment of the Second Republic. Again, revolutionary fervor coincided quite precisely with a solar maximum.

The tensions that led to the American Civil War mounted on an ascending solar cycle and finally exploded as that cycle reached its peak. The war actually broke out in April 1861 when Confederate forces attacked Fort Sumter in Charleston Bay. By 1866, the war was over— and the face of the sun was quiet again.

The twentieth century opened on a descending cycle which bottomed out in 1902. As the *Wright Flyer* bounced into the air at Kitty Hawk, we were entering Phase Two, the solar increase—and clearly a "new idea" swept through humanity. Other new ideas were brewing simultaneously. Like the French and the Americans before them, the Russian people were tiring of the excesses of the Czarist regime. The ill-fated first Russian revolution of 1905 coincided exactly with a solar maximum, as did the successful Bolshevik revolution of 1917.

True to form, World War I started in Phase Two of the sunspot cycle, peaked during the stormy sunspot maximum, and its final shots were fired during the descent toward minimum.

As we enter living memory, Chizhevsky's patterns seem, if anything, to become more vivid. The year 1923 marked a solar minimum. As the fabled Roaring Twenties got underway in earnest, the magnetic storms on the surface of the sun were also roaring toward a maximum which was centered around 1928. The frenzied stock market crash of 1929 occurred in the solar peak—but then solar activity plunged toward a minimum in 1933, as the world economy plunged into the Great Depression.

The road toward the Second World War waxed and waned in close synchronization with the solar cycle, but the war itself raises some interesting questions. The sunspot minimum of the early twenties found Adolph Hitler ignominiously defeated and locked in jail. Under the quiet sun, the social atmosphere was not yet ripe for his inflammatory ideas. Just a few years later, around the solar maximum, we find him living in a villa, a wealthy man. His infamous book, *Mein Kampf*, had sold ten million copies, riding the ascending solar cycle. As Chizhevsky put it, people were restive and "receptive to new ideas."

One might imagine that Hitler's perceived charisma would have waned as the solar storms moved toward the minimum of 1933. Actually, that was the year in which he seized power. Perhaps significantly, Hitler was immediately confronted by serious opposition from within his own party. He instigated the "blood purge" of 1934, murdering hundreds of political opponents, while the army and the judiciary passively looked on. Passivity can be dangerous, needless to say. And during the solar minima, there is often an atmosphere of, "Why bother?"

On schedule, Germany's annexation of Austria and conquest of Czechoslovakia—the real military beginning of World War II—coincided with a solar maximum. That is not surprising, based on what we've seen previously. More surprising is the fact that the second half of World War II was fought during a theoretically "tranquil" solar minimum. Obviously, a war is easier to start than to finish. While the violence of the last couple of years of World War II clearly contrast with Chizhevsky's formulas, one of the most vivid images in mind for capturing the flat spirit of the solar dive toward minimum is the picture of disheartened soldiers trudging through the mud and the snow in a war that would not end.

Peace came in 1945 in the solar minimum, but was followed two or three years later by the stormiest solar maximum since the American Revolution. In 1949, the Soviets detonated their first nuclear bomb and the horror of the Cold War was in full swing. In the United States, Joseph McCarthy began his rabid witch-hunt for "communists," and was not finally silenced until condemned by the U.S. Senate in late 1954—during the quieter, more balanced solar minimum of that year.

The highest solar peak ever recorded occurred in 1957. Appropriately, in that year humanity experienced the beginning of perhaps its greatest adventure with the launching of the Soviet Sputnik satellite and the onset of the space age. By early 1962, when the solar storms abated and our central star entered the relatively quiescent Phase Four, over seventy satellites and three human beings had been placed in orbit.

On a cultural level, we also find the birth of rock 'n' roll coinciding with this period of solar ascendancy. In June of 1955, Bill Haley and the Comets' "Rock Around the Clock" hit number one. Within the next year, they were eclipsed by the rise of Elvis Presley and the decades-long musical phenomenon which he set into motion. The frenzied excitement of kids dancing to "the devil's music" wonderfully reflects the wild, fiery excitement of the solar peak.

The year 1964 saw a quiet sun, but the climb started quickly as "Beatlemania" caught on. The years 1968-1970 were characterized by a long plateau of peak solar turbulence. Woodstock, the sexual revolution, the counterculture, the escalation of the war in Southeast Asia and the accompanying frenzy of protest at home, the first manned lunar landing—all unfolded during that extended maximum. Meanwhile, in China, Mao Tse-tung instituted the great witch hunt called the "Cultural Revolution" in May 1966. It continued in its most active form until the death of Lin Biao in 1971. As the sunspots faded, so did the passion.

Chizhevsky died in 1964, but he would certainly not have been surprised by the colorful, impassioned events of those years.

Another solar maximum occurred in 1979-1981. What happened? Once again, masses of people were excited by new leaders and new ideas, all gathering momentum in the final years of the 1970s. Ronald Reagan was elected president, riding the crest of a tidal wave of conservative reaction that roared across the country. Fundamentalist Christian fervor burst onto the scene after a long period of decline. "Pray TV" became a household word. Parallel events unfolded in the Islamic world with the rise of Ayatollah Khomeini and the explosion of Muslim fundamentalism, not to mention the rise of terrorism.

Our own times are, of course, the hardest to see clearly. The problem is compounded by the fact that the solar cycle is erratic. But the pattern is holding. As I write these words, in the very last month of the 1980s, the sun is roaring toward a maximum that may prove to be the fiercest one ever recorded. Appropriately, we find masses of people stirred into frantic, passionate motion. Under the charismatic influence of Mikhail Gorbachev, the Berlin Wall is being broken up for souvenirs. Marxist-Leninist governments are resigning every day. In the spring of 1989, coinciding closely with a record-breaking solar flare, the Chinese government crushed protests in Tiananmen Square.

You, reader, placed further down the time-line than me, undoubtedly understand the meaning of these events more precisely than I do. Still, even to me sitting in the midst of breaking news stories, it's clear that Chizhevsky's model is vindicated yet again.

Whatever is going on, the entire scenario should reach some sort of crescendo, for better or worse, in the early 1990s.

(Note: I wrote these words in late '89. As I finalize this manuscript in mid-'91, we've just fought another sunspot war: the clash with Iraq.)

"For better or worse." In many ways, that phrase represents the crux of Chizhevsky's speculations. His sunspot theory, apparently sound, is not absolutely deterministic. Like the proverbial blind man holding the elephant's tail, these considerations give us only one piece of the puzzle. Ultimately, sunspots appear to have a strong correlation with humanity's emotions and passions. Beyond that, they don't illuminate very much. The same peaks that parallel war and horror also sometimes parallel outpourings of art and science. The same lows that are associated with peace and tranquility can also reveal an environment in which a Hitler can quietly insinuate himself into the social structure. During the solar peak of the late sixties, America swung toward liberalism. With the following peak, we swung back to the Right. Who knows where the next one will carry us?

For our purposes, the critical point is that there appears to be a demonstrable relationship between humanity's mood and the solar cycle. Accepting the reality of that linkage is a far cry from buying into all the astrological arcana of Sun Signs, Moon Signs and Ascendants. Logically, the solar cycle's ties with history could be valid, while the rest of astrology could be hogwash. Still, once we allow ourselves to recognize the cogency of Chizhevsky's work, we've opened a door. We have accepted that there may be a direct relationship between cosmos and consciousness, and that each is reflected in the other.

And that notion is the foundation upon which astrology rests.

UPDATE, 2016

Well, when I wrote the words you just read, it was 1988 or 1989. Now it's 2016, twenty-seven years later. Time flies. As I mentioned in the introduction to this revised edition of *The Night Speaks*, I want to avoid tampering too much with the original text. Anybody can be brilliant in retrospect. I've put some literary polish on it—what author could resist that temptation? But this is the way the world looked to me back then, around my fortieth birthday. It doesn't look so different to me today really, at least in terms of astrology. But of course there's been a lot of water under the bridge historically since then.

I want to ask the obvious question: have the theories expounded by Aleksandr Leonidovich Chizhevsky continued to hold up to scrutiny? Have the last two or three decades reflected the same distinct pattern we investigated from 1730 through 1990? As before, you can easily judge for yourself—in fact, you can do so even more easily now since the times we are about to consider are modern, within the lifespans of most of my younger readers.

You were there. You know what it felt like.

We left off at about 1990. Consider this new graph, showing the sunspot cycle from 1984 to nearly the present.

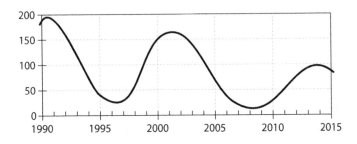

Clearly, the solar fires roared up to a powerful peak from 1989 through 1992. As we explored a little while ago, right on Chizhevsky's schedule, 1989 brought the fall of the Berlin Wall and essentially the end of Cold War. In 1990, the two Germanies—East and West—reunited. In 1991, the Union of Soviet Socialist Republics collapsed into fifteen separate states. The chaos continued. In August 1990, Saddam Hussein's armies invaded Kuwait, triggering a brief war in which he was quickly driven back. He famously "declared victory" and ran away. I remember reading that news story in an airport terminal—just "Iraq invades Kuwait," two hundred words on the bottom of the front page, as if it were no big deal. I remember getting a sinking feeling in my belly, thinking, "uh oh, this is going to be big."

It took a little while, but of course those intuitions proved prophetic.

Meanwhile, in 1988, as the solar cycle climbed toward its crescendo, a then-unknown Osama bin Laden formed a group called "al-Qaeda." At the peak of the cycle, in 1992, he was banished from his native Saudi Arabia for his rabble-rousing and moved his base to Sudan.

As is so often the case with history, these events only loom large and ominous when we are looking backward. At the time, nobody noticed.

Here is another example of that kind of phenomenon, although in this case a happier one. Ever heard of Sir Timothy John Berners-Lee? I hadn't either until I started researching these time-lines. In the words of Wikipedia, Berners-Lee "is an English computer scientist, best known as the inventor of the World Wide Web." He proposed an Internet-based information management system in March of 1989, and successfully demonstrated it that November. In Chizhevsky's summary of the solar increase, we read, "Exciting new ideas and charismatic spokespeople appear, planting seeds that quickly germinate into mass movements."

The World Wide Web and al-Qaeda are obviously two very different entities—but note how well Chizhevsky's words fit each of them. And of course one appeared in 1988 and the other in 1989, right on track with the sunspot cycle.

By the way, recall that Chizhevsky suggested a three-year rise in the sunspot cycle followed by two-year peak, then a three-year descent and a three-year bottom. A cursory glance at this graph shows the considerable variability in these solar cycles. Best to take Chizhevsky's number as ratios—and to take the ratios with a grain of salt.

The huge peak in 1992 brought two more developments. One was the terrible riots in Los Angeles, California, that resulted from cabdriver Rodney King being beaten by police. Unfortunately for the violent officers, the event was videotaped. The public explosion that followed left fifty-five people dead and a couple thousand injured, as well as vast swaths of property destruction. Passions ran high, as did the sunspots.

The second and final event I would like to underscore here at this solar peak is the 1992 passage of the Maastricht Treaty, which created the European Union. Quoting our earlier summary of Chizhevsky's theories about the solar maximum, "Everyone is excited, eager to respond *en masse* to leadership or inspiration, for better or worse." And Europe unites. Getting a bit out of historical sequence here, I cannot resist adding that as I write these words in July 2016, "Brexit" has just happened. The people of the United Kingdom just voted to leave the EU. No one presently knows what that event will ultimately mean, but the vote is widely framed as more emotional than logical—and the sunspot cycle seems to be just past a peak in 2014-15. Thus, the passions that created the European Union may also destroy it.

The merciless history of our species, needless to say, can make awfully depressing reading. But sometimes we get it right. Sometimes we seem to overcome our more bloody-minded, separative instincts and actually rise above ourselves. One of the finest examples in my mind of that encouraging human quality is the end of *apartheid* in South Africa. Before that happened, I could not envision a peaceful resolution of the tense injustices which dominated that society, with a vast, hopeless black majority under the thumb of a tiny, privileged white minority. It seemed like a detonation waiting for a spark. And yet, on April 27, 1994, as the solar cycle wound down, Nelson Mandela was elected president of South Africa. The revolution was, relatively speaking, bloodless—at least on the normal scale of such regime changes.

I can't help but think that the calmer, more reasonable energies of the solar minimum of 1994-1997 had something to do with that good news.

In a similarly peaceful vein, in 1997, right at the bottom of the minimum, the United Kingdom voluntarily gave Hong Kong back to China. Not everyone was happy—but all of the alternatives to that simple solution were perilous.

It is interesting to compare this peaceful turnover of Hong Kong to the 1982 Falklands War between the United Kingdom and Argentina—fought just past a solar maximum—when nine hundred people died.

Hong Kong and the Falklands: two far-flung British colonies, vestiges of colonialism—and fairly said, two very different situations—and yet one situation is settled via negotiation and another with blood, death, and hatred. To say the difference was "all because of sunspots" is foolishly reductionistic—but to ignore the solar cycle is to be blind to what is obviously emerging here as a major astrological influence on collective human behavior.

It is instructive, by the way, to look closely at our graph. Each cycle has a similar basic structure—oscillating peaks and troughs—but also its own unique form, much like human faces. The solar minimum of the mid-1990s descended gradually, then roared upward in a remarkably explosive ascent, starting from a deep bottom in 1997. You get the sense of something "bursting" to happen, something passionately demanding expression. That solar cycle peaked in 2000-2002. Of course, any American would immediately think of September 11, 2001, when the World Trade Center was destroyed. For all its horror, that frenzied moment stands as an indelible illustration of the mad face of the solar maximum.

The name Osama bin Laden is of course forever bound to that hard day. We encountered him already here once, seeing him riding the ascending solar cycle back in 1988, founding al-Qaeda. Ten years later, in February 1998, again on an ascending cycle, bin Laden issued a *fatwa* against the entire West "in the name of the World

Islamic Front for Jihad Against Jews and Crusaders." It declared the killing of North Americans and their allies an "individual duty for every Muslim."

At the time, bin Laden's brazen announcement wasn't headline material, but as the face of the sun roared back in fire, he took aim at the Twin Towers and claimed his dark place in history. "Charismatic leaders arise …"

Coinciding with that momentous peak in the sunspot cycle, the "War on Terror" began with the invasion of Afghanistan in 2001. The next year brought the terrible "Bali bombings" and riots in the Indian state of Gujarat that left over a thousand people dead. The Guantanamo Bay detention center was established then too. In March 2003, with the sunspots still blazing, the invasion of Iraq began.

As I write these words, these events are only a little over a decade old. Unless you are a young person reading this book down the road into the future somewhere, you remember them. You lived through them.

That is what a sunspot peak feels like.

Remember, though: even though the world tends to boil over at such times, often there are "exciting new ideas" emerging and taking hold. Let's not let the bad news entirely eclipse them. In 2000, the International Space Station began operation—and provided a counterbalance to the divisiveness evident in the grim headlines. Humans *can* cooperate with each other across cultural boundaries. The enormous, multi-nation effort that has culminated in our first "permanent" address in space proves that. In 2001, both Wikipedia and the African Union were founded. Good things too—but still, I, for one, would not want to live through that grim period a second time. In many ways, that solar peak of 2000-2002 marked the end of the world of relative freedom in which I grew up. I will have more to say about that later on in Chapter Ten as we put these last two solar peaks in the context of yet another, very different but even more massive celestial rhythm: the epochal, world-changing alignment of Uranus and Neptune.

For now, let's follow the quieting sun down to the trough of the solar minimum that ran through 2007, 2008, and 2009.

2005 and the solar decline brought the Kyoto Protocol. At last there emerged some hope for international cooperation on atmospheric carbon emissions and subsequent climate disruption. It was at least a start. In the same year, as the solar energies began to flatten, the Irish Republican Army ended its long war in Northern Ireland, while Israel withdrew from Gaza—only to invade again in 2008, then to withdraw once more, right at the bottom of the solar cycle, in 2009.

Meanwhile, war dragged on in Iraq, as did terrorism across the globe. This persistence of trouble despite a quieting Sun reminds me of World War II, which as we saw earlier ran on through a declining solar cycle, seemingly fueled by its own nightmarish momentum. People are less impassioned and engaged, but unable to withdraw from the nightmare they have set into motion. Trouble is famously easier to start than to stop.

The world economy crashed in 2007 and bottomed out in 2008, right at the bottom of the solar cycle. We were "out of fuel" in more ways than one.

As the sun flickered back to life in 2009-2010 and we entered Chizhevsky's solar increase, the prediction is that "social energies begin to coalesce." On December 17, 2010, Mohamed Bouazizi set himself on fire in Tunisia in protest of his treatment at the hands of corrupt petty officials there. That was the trigger that sparked the series of explosive events across the Islamic world now known as "the Arab Spring." It peaked in 2011 with initially successful popular revolutions not only in Tunisia, but also in Egypt and Libya, not to mention failed ones in Bahrain and Yemen. In a somewhat different vein, the Syrian civil war began.

Meanwhile in the Western world, the "Occupy" movement, protesting the perceived injustices symbolized by Wall Street, got started in New York City. That was in September 2011. By October, Occupy protests had happened or were currently happening in nearly a thousand cities in the United States, as well as in eighty-two other countries. Again, people were responding to the rising fires on the face of the sun ninety-three million miles away.

In 2012, at the solar maximum, Israel once more invaded the Gaza Strip—that beleaguered land providing such a crystalline mirror for the sunspot cycle. The solar minimum had supplied a brief respite, but as the sun began to roar, again so did the twinned human passions: rage and fear.

The "Black Lives Matter" movement got its start in 2013 after security guard George Zimmerman was acquitted for killing black teenager, Trayvon Martin. The movement gained enormous momentum with police shootings and documented brutality toward African Americans in 2014 and 2015. It is illustrative to recall the parallels with the Rodney King riots in Los Angeles back in 1992, also at a solar maximum.

One of Chizhevsky's central observations is that the solar rise and maximum both bring us new, charismatic leaders to whom people respond with enthusiasm and strong feelings. A luminous illustration of that notion is the election of Jorge Mario Bergoglio, in 2013, to become Pope Francis I. He has very much shaken up the conservative order of the Roman Catholic Church and brought many new congregants into the fold. We might also mention Edward Snowden, who in the same year went public with many of the darker secrets of the United States' National Security Agency. Some swear by him as a saint and some swear at him as a traitor. Either way, he certainly fits Chizhevsky's model.

In June 2014, right around the apparent peak of the current cycle, the "Islamic State," often called ISIS, which was blitzkreiging across Syria and Iraq in seemingly unstoppable fashion, declared a caliphate. Meanwhile, in the same year, protests in Ukraine triggered a revolution and the overthrow of the president—which led to Russia moving in and annexing Crimea. Soon the Western world too felt it was teetering close to edge of one of its ultimate nightmares: war with Russia. The sunspots were exploding; so were human passions: once again, the same pattern.

Because of the innate element of unpredictability in the sunspot cycle, it is unlike any other astrological force. All the rest of the planetary cycles can be foreseen with accuracy. Sunspots, on the other hand, only work reliably in the present or past tense. As we look forward in time, we can only make guesses based on previous patterns. As we mentioned near the beginning of this chapter, even though solar cycles average about eleven years in length, there were once two peaks only seven years apart. Another time, seventeen years separated them.

So where are we now in the cycle?

For the reasons just described, it is difficult to say with certainty. Probably the peak can be understood to have occurred in about 2012-2014. It was still high in 2015—as history amply reflects. That year brought the *Charlie Hebdo* horror in Paris, with terrorists murdering cartoonists. Around the same time, in Nigeria, "Boko Haram" massacred more than two thousand human beings, while claiming alliance with the Islamic State. In late 2015, there was a terrorist-inspired mass murder in San Bernardino, California, leaving fourteen people dead. America was again shaken. Then, in June 2016, Omar Mateen, claiming affiliation with ISIS, walked into a gay-friendly nightclub in Orlando, Florida, and murdered 49 people.

I am writing these words in the middle of 2016, so more water has flowed under the bridge since *Charlie Hebdo,* San Bernardino and Orlando. But I am going to quit the historical analysis now. It is tempting to bring us up to date—the rise of Donald Trump calls out for some sunspot perspective, as do the various, more current, examples of rampant "overstimulation" around the world.

One reason I want to stop here is simply because I am aware of how difficult it is to see our own times clearly. A second reason, as I mentioned a moment ago, is that exactly where we are in the sunspot cycle at the moment is fuzzy.

There is a third reason, though, and it may be the most important one of all. The sun is behaving very weirdly.

WHAT IS GOING ON WITH THE SUN?

A quick look at the graph of sunspot activity since 1984 reveals an obvious fact: the current peak is a very low one. Since the 1992 peak, the energy has been stepping down. Going back to the earlier sunspot cycle graph, one can easily see that since records began to be kept with some accuracy in about 1730, there have been very high peaks and very low peaks—the intensity of the solar maximum has always been variable, in other words. And who knows? The next peak, predicted for about 2025, could be the highest one in history—or not happen at all. Or happen at the "wrong" time. We simply cannot predict sunspots with total confidence.

What we do know is that this present solar maximum is the *lowest one in over a century.*

There's more. Solar peaks are often "spiky" rather than smooth curves. As you can see from our two graphs, it is not unusual to get a "double-peaked" maximum. The present maximum, even though it is very mild, reflects that two-headed pattern. There was a distinct peak in March 2012 and another in April 2014. That is not a rare thing—but this time it had an unprecedented feature: the second peak was higher than the first. That particular phenomenon had never been observed before.

Does it portend anything? Again, no one really knows.

In early June 2016, just six weeks ago as I write, the face of the sun went completely blank for four days. It looked exactly like the sun at the bottom of a minimum. But it is too soon for that—or is it? We appear to be experiencing a strangely precipitous drop-off from the solar maximum. The next minimum is predicted for 2019-2020. Will we get there sooner?

History holds a foggy mirror before us. There is suggestive evidence that sunspot activity was quite minimal from about 1645 to 1715, the so-called "Maunder Minimum." We must take this statement with some caution since it happened long before the time of rigorous, consistent observation of solar phenomena. It is, in other words, a classic case of trying to distinguish the "absence of evidence" from the "evidence of absence."

One strong argument in favor of the reality of the Maunder Minimum is that it coincides with the very center of a longer period of subnormal temperatures that is usually called "the Little Ice Age." Advancing glaciers destroyed villages in the Swiss Alps. Rivers and canals in Britain and northern Europe froze solid enough for ice-skating. The Norse settlements in Greenland had to be abandoned. Sea ice surrounded Iceland, extending far out to sea, closing its harbors.

Less fire on the Sun, less warmth on the Earth? It holds together logically. Some climatologists favor different explanations—and again, the lack of hard data about the actual sunspot numbers stymies more definitive inquiry. My guess is that the Maunder Minimum was real.

The Sun, in other words, can sometimes lose its spots.

Our central star is about five billion years old. Three centuries is only the blink of an eye compared to that gargantuan timescale. If, for some unknown reason, the sunspot cycle became dormant for seventy years three centuries ago, there is of course no reason to imagine that it could not be happening again now.

The peaks in the sunspot cycle are currently trending downward. Of that there is no doubt. They have been doing that since the high crescendo of the early 1990s. Is that reduction in solar activity a fluke, or is something more fundamental happening? Are we heading for another "Maunder Minimum?" Or will the cycle spring back in power next time around?

Only time will tell—but not much time. We should know within the decade.

At the close of this chapter in the original edition of this book, I summarized the core point of my writing about the sunspot cycle in these words: "For our purposes, the critical point is that there appears to be a demonstrable relationship between humanity's mood and the solar cycle."

That remains the pivotal argument of this chapter.

Human history is wild and woolly. Craziness, mayhem, brilliance, and even wisdom can strike at any moment. But it is hard for me to imagine any open-minded person reading these last several pages and not being convinced that the sunspot cycle and human affairs are at least somewhat entrained. To me, that point is easily seen—and to refute it would require tortured rationalization. The sunspot cycle plainly underlies what you see in daily news. Once we recognize that fact, we are still many miles away from believing in "Leo" and "Gemini," but we have accepted that there may be a mirroring relationship between celestial and terrestrial affairs.

And that is the core principle upon which ultimately astrology rests.

3

DENIAL

In her collection of futuristic tales, *Visible Light*, C.J. Cherryh writes, "Even to believe we can't know is a system. Maybe we can know the universe. Maybe there is an answer. It's dangerous to assume there isn't."

She's correct, of course. "Unbelief" is just as arbitrary, just as much a religion, as belief itself.

While much of astrology is relatively concrete and specific, and thus subject to rational evaluation, its philosophical foundation is not. Ultimately, the philosophy behind the system rests upon a single belief: the conviction that the universe is inherently meaningful. More commonly, this principle is expressed another way: that the heavens, specifically the planets, symbolize human realities. But symbolism implies meaning, and as soon as we accept that meaning is inherent to the structure of the cosmos, we have entered mysterious and subversive territory.

Subversive to what?

To the mechanistic assumptions of Big Science.

To the God-is-in-Heaven and Heaven-is-Elsewhere assumptions upon which Big Religion is founded.

To the existentialist assumptions of much of modern art and modern literature, not to mention modern psychiatric theory.

In short, the notion that the physical universe is meaningful, even purposeful, and that it is telling us something personal, undercuts a large part of the unspoken mythology of modern culture. It runs counter to nearly everything most of us have been brought up to believe.

A few lines earlier in *Visible Light*, Cherryh suggests, "It's so easy to take what others give us. Gifts are so hard to say no to."

And what is the gift we are offered? The gift of life in a realm without meaning or purpose, governed by cold physical laws. Not very appealing emotionally—but it is remarkable how emotional people often become in defending their right to that emptiness. That seems to be especially true of those people who are most heavily invested in maintaining the modern world view: the so-called "rationalists," the conventional scientists, and all those who model their characters on them.

In the previous chapter, I attempted to persuade you that there are convincing, almost inescapable, reasons to accept the reality of at least one astrological effect—the correlation of the sunspot cycle with the shape of history. Soon we'll be encountering more evidence in support of astrology, this time regarding actual planetary linkages with individuals. But first, let's explore another territory: the pervasive, and in large part irrational, opposition to astrology ... a foaming-at-the-mouth opposition which functions in the academic world of science almost as a state religion.

THE GREAT DEBATE

In the fall of 1986, at Towson University in Maryland, Mary Ellen Glass was scheduled to teach a course on the Fundamentals of Astrology. The Department of Physical Sciences got wind of it and circulated a petition demanding that the class be canceled. Since Glass was under contract, the situation was knotty. She agreed to withdraw on the condition that "a formal dialogue" take place "between an astrological panel of her choosing and a panel of representatives from the Physics department."

At first, rather incredibly, the physicists refused to debate anyone except Glass herself, alone. She stuck to her guns, protesting that "four against one does not suggest an effective dialogue."

Eventually, on June 4, 1987, four physicists squared off against four astrologers.

When the dust settled, the "Great Debate," as it has come to be known in the folklore of the astrological community, ended well for the astrologers. According to Susan Blevins, reporting in the newsletter of the Association for Astrological Networking, July 1987, when the moderator asked for a show of hands as to which side presented the more cogent argument, "about two-thirds of the assembly" supported the astrologers, including "a good percentage from the 'scientific' side of the room."

In this case, the result was almost a foregone conclusion. The physicists had blundered badly, not so much in disbelieving astrology, but in allowing themselves to be swept into a debate titled "Resolution: Astrology is Appropriate as a University Course Offering." In her opening statement, Mary Ellen Glass quoted directly from the

Towson University's own promotional literature: "Higher education must introduce students to the range of knowledge and ways of knowing that have shaped human experience in the past, present and potentially for the future."

Given the pervasiveness of some form of astrological thought in virtually every society that has ever existed, the physicists' position was terribly weak. Even if there were absolutely nothing objectively true about astrology, the idea that it has played a wide role in the world's history, art, mythology and religion is completely and totally inescapable. On that basis alone it certainly merited inclusion in the curriculum.

Yet the physicists didn't see that. These otherwise rational people, through a seemingly obvious logical gaffe, placed themselves in a vulnerable, and ultimately embarrassing, position.

Why were they so upset by a simple astrology class? Evidently, the idea fired some neurons for them, canceling their typical detachment and objectivity. What was it about astrology that so bothered them?

These questions, as we will soon discover, are far more interesting and far more serious than they may appear on the surface.

SCIENCE BY DECREE

As a society, we are often bamboozled into thinking of scientists as a dispassionate lot, coolly sifting nuggets of truth from streams of data. Often the process actually works that way, but rarely so when the subject is the possibility of any celestial influence upon human experience. There, science more often operates with its eyes closed, seeing nothing but its own attitude.

The late Bart J. Bok, an astronomer who once taught at Harvard, was an ardent foe of astrology. Yet he never studied the subject. "At one time I thought seriously of becoming personally involved in statistical tests of astrological predictions," he stated, "but I abandoned this plan as a waste of time unless someone could first show me that there was some sort of physical foundation for astrology."

Bok's disbelief was his own business, and certainly no one could rightfully compel him to investigate an area in which he had little interest. The problem is that, claiming to speak for science, he spearheaded a rancorous, and ultimately groundless, attack on astrology and astrologers.

At Bok's instigation, an anti-astrology "manifesto" appeared in the *Humanist* magazine in late 1975. Some excerpts: "Scientists in a variety of fields have become concerned about the increased acceptance of astrology in many parts of the world ... Those who wish to believe in astrology should realize that there is no scientific foundation for its tenets ... It is simply a mistake to imagine that the forces exerted by stars and planets at the moment of birth can in any way shape our futures ... We believe that the time has come to challenge directly and forcefully the pretentious claims of astrological charlatans."

One hundred ninety-two scientists signed the manifesto. Nineteen of them were Nobel Laureates. Many had recognizable, authoritative names: Linus Pauling, Fred Hoyle, Konrad Lorenz, B.F. Skinner. None of them had done any significant research relevant to the document they signed. No studies were quoted, let alone conducted. Paul Feyerabend, author of Against Method, later wrote, "The judgment of the '192 leading scientists' rests on an antediluvian anthropology, on ignorance of more recent results in their own fields (astronomy, biology, and the connection between the two) as well as on a failure to perceive the implications of results they do know." Significantly, he adds, "It shows the extent to which scientists are prepared to assert their authority even in areas in which they have no knowledge whatsoever."

What's going on here? We can plainly see a pervasive anti-astrology bias in the scientific community. Always that bias is presented as a "scientific objection," as though a kind-hearted Mr. Wizard were patiently explaining to us the improbability of our ever meeting Santa Claus.

Yet is the anti-astrology bias really so objective? More, it seems, lies behind many scientists' aversion to the symbolic universe than a simple lack of data.

During the "Great Debate" at Towson State, Philip Ianna, co-author of the anti-astrology *Gemini Syndrome*, objected that there is "demonstrably no evidence that astrology works." To which Dr. Lee Lehman offered this delightful reply: "… If all courses at the university have to be empirically based, would you be prepared to defend the empirical basis of a course on Corsage Craft? Could you cite any studies showing the relative values of one form of corsage-making to another?"

Her argument is entertaining, but it also runs deeper than it appears. Simply said, much that is meaningful and worthwhile in life has little to do with logic, reason, or analysis.

Of all the many areas of human experience that have one foot beyond the pale of deductive rationality, why is it that astrology elicits such a vehement roar from scientists? A lot of people believe in angels. The scientists leave them alone. Many Christians believe that Jesus rose from the dead and that bread and wine turn literally to flesh and blood in the Eucharist. Have "192 leading scientists" ever banded together to indicate their doubts about any of that?

Why is astrology always the target? Why not Sasquatch?

Flushing out the ghosts that lurk behind this strangely impassioned behavior is our goal in the following chapter. But first let's consider the story of an elfin-eyed Frenchman and his former wife, who for four decades haunted the House of Science.

MICHEL AND FRANCOISE
GAUQUELIN

In the astrological community, they stand on the left hand of God. Outside that community, the Gauquelins' name has about the same recognition value as that of the Malagasy ambassador. What they have done, in a nutshell, is to demonstrate in rigidly scientific terms that the positions of the planets at a person's birth are associated with the shape of his or her subsequent career.

For a full treatment of their work, there is probably no better source than Michel Gauquelin's own book, *Birthtimes*. Space limitations allow me only a relatively brief summary here.

In the early 1950s, before the age of home computers, the Gauquelins laboriously assembled birth data on 576 professors of medicine, set up their birthcharts, and proceeded to analyze the results. "Suddenly, I was presented with an extraordinary fact," writes Michel. "My doctors were not born under the same skies as the common run of humanity. They had chosen to come into the world much more often during roughly the two hours following the rise and culmination of two planets, Mars and Saturn. Moreover, they tended to 'avoid' being born following the rise and culmination of the planet Jupiter."

The two researchers repeated their test, using a new sample of 508 more physicians. The results were exactly the same. Taken together, the statistical probability against the pattern being random was literally about a million to one.

In the following years, the Gauquelins continued their research, investigating the astrological correlates of many different professions. A telling discovery in their work has been that the planetary principles emerge statistically only when applied to people who have been successful in their professions, not just to average practitioners in the fields. (Success, of course, is tough to define rigorously. The Gauquelins' method has been to use only those subjects who merit inclusion in "Who's Who" kinds of books for each job category.) It seems that when people choose professions to which they are astrologically suited, they are more likely to function with high levels of effectiveness and success—an insight with clear implications regarding the practical value of astrological counsel.

Jupiter, in traditional astrology, symbolizes expansiveness, playfulness, and optimism. The Gauquelins demonstrated statistically its linkage to the charts of successful actors and playwrights, politicians, military leaders, top executives and journalists. They found it obscure in the birthcharts of scientists and, as we mentioned above, physicians.

Saturn traditionally represents realism, self-discipline, and caution, while threatening a constriction of joy and imagination. The Gauquelins demonstrated its association with the charts of successful scientists and physicians. They found it far less prominent in the birthcharts of actors, journalists, writers and painters.

Mars, astrology's "war god," symbolizes competitiveness, the capacity to function under stress, and the human capacity for violence. The Gauquelins' results link it to the charts of successful physicians, military leaders, sports champions, and executives. They found it underrepresented in the birthcharts of painters, musicians and writers.

Anyone can make wild assertions and claim they are scientific. Were the methods employed by the Gauquelins flawed? Did they simply "cheat," as some of their detractors have implied? Certainly, as we will soon see, they encountered a predictable pattern of resistance to their work on the part of the scientific community. But they convinced Hans Eysenck. He is a respected "hard" psychologist from the University of London Institute of Psychiatry, best known as the originator of the Eysenck Personality Questionnaire, which is one of the more widely employed psychological inventories. After reviewing the Gauquelins' work, Eysenck wrote, "I think it may be said that, as far as objectivity of observation, statistical significance of differences, verification of hypothesis, and reliability are concerned, there are few sets of data in psychology which could compete with these observations. Full details of all the persons included in these studies are given in the voluminous publications of the Gauquelins, and I have checked a small random sample of easily accessible ones ... I think we must admit that there is something here that requires explanation."

Tellingly, Eysenck added, "Emotionally, I would prefer the Gauquelins' results not to hold, but rationally, I must accept that they do."

Given the anti-astrology climate in academia, Hans Eysenck took a risk in speaking up. Yet even he, by his own admission, was infected with the same emotional "virus" that led the 192 "leading scientists" to compromise the most fundamental axiom of the scientific method: to let truth, not sentiment, be the criterion by which facts are established. Like those who signed the *Humanist* manifesto, Eysenck had an emotional bias against astrology. But Eysenck's virus was merely a headache; it didn't distort his reason.

Watch what happens when the Gauquelins stumble into the typhoid ward.

CSICOP

The Committee for the Scientific Investigation of Claims of the Paranormal (CSICOP) was launched in 1976. Its founder, Paul Kurtz, was the editor of the *Humanist* at the time of the publication of the infamous anti-astrology edict. The avowed purpose of the Committee is to debunk astrology, parapsychology, and other "outdated mythologies"—a goal which immediately casts a strange light on any claim to open-minded, neutral scientific investigation.

In reality, CSICOP functioned with a species of bone-headed self-righteousness reminiscent of the Holy Inquisition.

Alongside the *Humanist*'s manifesto, one Lawrence J. Jerome, a "scientific writer," published an article dismissing the Gauquelins' work on technical grounds. The criticisms were far-fetched; Michel Gauquelin dealt with them effectively in a letter published in the following issue. Paul Kurtz then brought in Marvin Zelen, a professor of statistical sciences at Harvard. Zelen agreed that Jerome's anti-Gauquelin arguments did not hold water. He then proposed a test that would settle once and for all whether there was a "Mars effect," as the observed astrological pattern came to be called. He suggested that birth data be collected for a sample of people who were not sports champions, but who happened to be born on the same days as the athletes upon whom that part of the Gauquelins' research was based. The idea was that if there were some non-astrological force behind the Mars-rising-or-culminating pattern among athletes, it ought to affect everyone else born on the same days as well.

Enter CSICOP.

The "Zelen test" was conducted under the Committee's aegis. It showed clearly, as Michel Gauquelin wrote, "that non-champions born under the same conditions as champions, do not display the Mars effect, and that this effect can be observed only among the champions."

But in an article about the Zelen test which was published in the *Humanist*, the truth was distorted. The female athletes, who gave the clearest demonstration of the Mars effect, were eliminated. The distinction between champions and non-champions was obfuscated. And finally, the Gauquelins' honesty in gathering the test data was questioned.

Dr. Elisabeth Scott, one of the signatories of the original manifesto, was concerned. After seeing a pre-publication version of the article, she phoned Paul Kurtz and his CSICOP associates, urging them to take a more balanced view. Later, she wrote to Kurtz, "I understand that the paper was published virtually unchanged. What I would like to do now is to publish a short note or, even a letter, stating clearly what I think your error is. Is this a possibility? Would you publish such a note?'

No note ever appeared in the *Humanist*.

Petty wars followed, with the Gauquelins persisting. CSICOP tried twisting the results, and when that failed, they resorted to ignoring proposals for further research. Finally, in late 1981, the guillotine fell. Dennis Rawlins, one of the founders of CSICOP and no friend of astrology, published an article titled "sTarbaby." In the opening paragraph, he characterized CSICOP as "a group of would-be debunkers who bungled their major investigation, falsified the results, covered up their error and gave the boot to a colleague who threatened to tell the truth." That colleague was Rawlins himself.

Dennis Rawlins, an astronomer, had done all the mathematical work for the Zelen test. The only piece of the puzzle that he did not hold in his own hands was the actual assembly of the list of athletes. That had been left to Paul Kurtz.

Michel Gauquelin has questioned the authenticity of that list; in *Birthtimes*, he writes, "My own analysis of the structure of the data had pinpointed some anomalies in this particular area, casting doubt on its objectivity."

Further mud for the waters: according to Rawlins, Kurtz had sent him "the first set of data secretly, saying that he wished a private advance look at how the computation was going to come out."

Rawlins complied; as he neared the end of the mathematical work, he informed Kurtz that the Gauquelins' work was being vindicated. Kurtz then "phoned me up and said oops, we accidentally missed a lot of names." Inexplicably, those eighty-two "forgotten" names showed an extreme "anti-Mars-effect" strong enough to neutralize the emerging pattern.

It is difficult to escape the impression of a deliberate distortion on Kurtz's part. This indeed was Rawlins' conclusion.

"I am convinced that Rawlins' report is certainly true in broad outline and probably true in every detail." So wrote R.A. McConnell, a professor of biophysics at the University of Pittsburgh, in a letter he circulated to all the fellows of CSICOP. He added, "One scientist has summarized it in this way: Rawlins has uncovered the biggest scandal in the history of rationalism."

What can we conclude?

That the Gauquelins demonstrated there are rational, statistical, reasons to accept the notion that our psyches interact with the larger cosmos in ways that can be termed "astrological."

That, despite claims to the contrary, there is indeed scientific evidence in support of at least some astrological principles.

And finally, that there exists a pervasive taboo among many so-called "rational" people, against taking seriously the idea of the Symbolic Universe.

4

GROANS

The world in a grain of sand: sometimes the tiniest gesture can convey a cosmos of information. A glance, a touch, a moment of eye contact … suddenly the Book of Life is opened, read, memorized, digested. Ask anyone who's ever fallen in love.

Here is an example of such a gesture, though it has little to do with tenderness.

During the CSICOP investigation of the Gauquelins' data, Dennis Rawlins and Paul Kurtz were in touch by phone. Kurtz, as we saw in the previous chapter, was monitoring the ongoing attempt to prove that there was no Mars effect in the charts of sports champions. Rawlins writes, "At one point (after 120 names), I told Kurtz by phone that the key sector score was now 22%. *He groaned.*"

The numbers indicated that the Gauquelins were vindicated. Significantly, it was at this point that Kurtz came up with his list of "forgotten" names displaying a phenomenal anti-Mars effect—the move which finally prompted Rawlins to blow the whistle.

But Kurtz groaned. That is the gesture upon which our epistle hangs. That simple, forgettable, forgivable human act: a groan. What did it convey? Sorrow. Loss. Frustration. Anger, maybe.

And why did he groan? Because astrology was *working.*

The Myth of Science, as we mentioned in the previous chapter, suggests that one investigates all phenomena with dispassion. Calmly, logically, one attempts to establish principles and actualities. In other words, there is no room for wishes and fears … at least in theory. In practice, of course, people are human. Neither you nor I nor Paul Kurtz can ever really leave our hearts out of the equation entirely. Sadly, hilariously, perhaps inevitably, we are all "rooting" for the triumph of a certain version of the universe. Racists enjoy meeting people of other genetic backgrounds who display obvious defects of character. Cynics appreciate it when a preacher is caught with his pants down. And many members of the First Church of the Mechanical Cosmos light up when astrology fails.

But this time astrology did not fail. And that bothered Paul Kurtz. It apparently bothered him enough that he willingly risked his career and reputation in order to obscure the truth.

As an astrologer, it would be easy simply to "judge" CSICOP and to glory in their humiliation. But I want to go deeper than that. I want to recognize that there is a little Inquisitor inside me, and maybe one inside you too. I don't want to torture that Inquisitor; I want to understand him. Which leads us to one critical question: Why is the astrological principle threatening to so many otherwise rational people? Scientists abandon long-standing methods. Lies are told. People compromise themselves, make themselves look foolish, all in an effort to ensure that the chaos-monster of astrology be safely confined within a cage of ridicule.

Why?

Ask a typical rationalist. You will probably hear the voice of sweet reason: "There's absolutely no evidence ... astrology is a pseudo-science ... charlatans and their victims ..."

But none of those statements is true. As we have seen, there is plenty of evidence, even in scientific terms, for the notion that consciousness and cosmos interact. And we have only scratched the surface. There is a lot more such evidence, and we will be exploring some of it in the final three chapters of this book.

Push one of astrology's critics who has fallen into that superstitious pit, face him or her with the disconcerting facts, and the veneer of dispassionate reason collapses, revealing denial, mockery maybe even the bones of a CSI-COP-style fiasco. In other words, when we press our case with those who vehemently oppose astrology, we begin to observe "psychological phenomena" in them.

Or psychopathological phenomena, to be utterly precise.

We encounter Kurtz's groan.

THE FEAR OF ASTROLOGY

Criticism, in calculated doses, can be a tonic. Without it, falsehoods and megalomania flourish. This goes for systems of thought as much as it does for people. Astrology needs criticism, prospers from it, can stand up to it. There is, in my opinion, an awful vacuum where astrology's own internal, self-administered criticism should be. Throughout much of the craft's history, astrologers have displayed a disturbing tendency to accept principles on the strength of "ancient authorities" without testing them. Even today, most astrological writers base their books on established traditions tempered by personal experience. (My own *Sky* trilogy, as proud as I am of it, is no exception.) New ideas can be accepted and incorporated into widespread use merely as a result of a writer's eloquence or personal charisma.

This, of course, is not only unfortunate, but dangerous.

Here is one tempting explanation for this lack of internal criticism within the astrological community: the deficit is balanced by a superfluity of criticism from everywhere else. Always, astrologers are on the defensive. Always, we are caricatured, represented as flakes, thrown into the same box with whatever bizarre claims are appearing in that week's grocery store tabloid.

And who does the criticizing? Typically people who know almost nothing about astrology, but who nonetheless claim to speak on behalf of Rationality ... or of God.

I personally feel that astrology could use some healthy, knowledgeable self-criticism. Michel Gauquelin himself, while he was alive, provided a considerable amount of that. While his work certainly supports the core assumptions of astrology, there are divergences between his discoveries and the astrological tradition.

My own aim here is different; I want to do something that has only rarely been done. I want to criticize the critics.

My premise, in a nutshell, is this: there exists a pervasive perceptual bias among those "normal," "rational" people who feel emotionally compelled to criticize astrology. The bias functions on an unconscious level, driving them towards otherwise inexplicable behaviors—behaviors that are characterized by denial, anger, inappropriate assumption of authority, and illogic. The trigger for these bad behaviors is broad, broader by far than astrology. In fact, it embraces approximately half of the total spectrum of experience available to human consciousness. The triggering stimulus is the suggestion that rational processes might in any way be influenced by irrational or "trans-rational" processes.

To keep my argument within the bounds of this book's subject matter, I will label this disorder *Astrophobia*. But, as we will discover, astrology's fate is linked to the fate of much else that, at least once, was held precious in this world.

DUALITY

Among those who can read without moving their lips, the idea that the brain has two hemispheres is today common knowledge. While the linkage of the right hemisphere with intuition and the left hemisphere with logic is a relatively new discovery, the idea behind it is prehistoric. Light and dark, sun and moon, hot and cold, dry and wet—humanity could hardly help building cosmologies around duality, so pervasive is it in all our perceptions.

As the fish knows little of the ocean, it is difficult for us to know much of the culture in which we live. But I suspect that a thousand years from now, our distant offspring will view us as a curiously half-witted lot, looking at the world through only half our brains, militantly ignoring fifty percent of our intelligence.

As intuitives and symbol readers, our species is currently on about the same intellectual level as something growing in the back of your refrigerator.

This bias in human awareness is like a dark iceberg with many separate pinnacles. Compare the average income of poets with that of stockbrokers. Consider mom's and dad's joy when Susie makes A's on her report card. Compare that to their joy when she tracks mud into the house, speaking glowingly of how she thinks she might have heard the stars whisper.

Throughout the mythology of our culture, we observe the same pattern: the left brain is elevated; the right brain, denigrated.

Nowhere is this split so evident as in the classical gender roles, and the values assigned to them. Turbulent water: who knows the truth of how men and women differ? Our primal natures and five thousand years of social scripting: put them both in the Cuisinart®, punch the button, and out comes a modern human. But certainly women, either by nature or by programming, have traditionally been identified with our intuitive right brain/left hand, leaving the "more valuable stuff" to men.

What does this have to do with astrology? Everything. The same social disorder that has damaged our access to the right brain has also damaged astrology, and for much the same reasons. While it would be wrong to bar men from the intuitive part of human consciousness, I do feel that the present astrological renaissance is riding the same historical wave that ushered in feminism. Certainly the two phenomena have coincided in time. And without doubt, there are far more women working with astrological symbolism today than there are men.

Riane Eisler, in her earth-shaking book *The Chalice and the Blade*, makes a convincing case for a return to a Neolithic value-system in which she believes male and female were seen in complementary terms. At one point, she writes, "It of course makes eminent sense that the earliest depiction of divine power in human form should have been female rather than male. When our ancestors began to ask the eternal questions (Where do we come from before we are born? Where do we go after we die?), they must have noted that life emerges from the body of a woman. It would have been natural for them to image the universe as an all-giving Mother."

Robert Bly, in his essay "I Came Out of the Mother Naked," agrees. He wrote, "Just as every adult was once inside the Mother, every society was once inside the Great Mother … Archaeologists have found hundreds of statues in caves and settlement ruins during the last thirty years … and they have never found a statue of the Great Father—the statues found, all over the world, are statues of the Great Mother."

Bly adds, "When men took over, they did their best to suppress all memories of the hostile mothers and the long age of woman power … Only what was in memory remained: *astrology, the great intellectual triumph of the Mother civilization*, is left, the Tarot psychology, the I CHING, and fairy tales all over the world (emphasis mine)."

Eisler and Bly, of course, are writing of gender. But their thoughts must inevitably be extended to embrace even more fundamental territory: the two hemispheres of the human brain, or to be a little less clinical about it, our "heads" and our "hearts."

More than females have been oppressed. Our ability to feel, our capacity for transcendence, even our creativity—all have been damaged and degraded.

The process is violent. Riane Eisler makes a chillingly convincing case for the way improvements in the status of women, always linked to resurgences of art and spirituality, have historically also served as superb predictors of war. The "Blade" fears the "Chalice," and knows that its "feminine virtues" can never prosper under the exigencies of bloody conflict. The madness of our age—this schism— is maintained at extravagant expense. "Men," as Robert Bly writes, "… have fought for centuries against the Great Mother, burning her temples and killing her priests, while shamans dressed as women struggled hard to absorb her magical power, castrated priests to absorb her religious power, wigged judges to absorb her judicial power."

Which bring us directly back to Paul Kurtz's groan.

The *Astrophobia* that we observe distorting the behavior of even Nobel Laureates is a tiny thing, a whisper in the chorus. But it is cut from the same cloth that impoverishes women and poets, that shames gentle men, that gives us war and rape, and the cult of the bleeding hero.

And who displays the symptoms of *Astrophobia* most vividly? Who groans? The High Priests of the brain's left hemisphere. Again and again, it is the less imaginative scientists, the "rationalists" who feel compelled to attack astrology. Faced with the claim that their sacred logical processes might in any way be influenced by "mysterious forces," they erupt.

A few lines ago, I quoted Robert Bly's reference to astrology as "the great intellectual triumph of the Mother Civilization." Let's think about that idea. It is the linchpin of our argument.

THANKS MOM

As I lived with the ideas Riane Eisler expresses in *The Chalice and the Blade,* I was struck by how differently the universe appeared when viewed through the metaphorical filter of a nurturing "Goddess" rather than a judging, male "God."

Eisler writes that these "… images of the Goddess … express a view of the world in which the primary purpose of art, and of life, was not to conquer, pillage and loot but to cultivate the earth and provide the material and spiritual wherewithal for a satisfying life."

In sharp contrast with the harsh, retributive spirit of Jehovah, under the Goddess, "the primary function of the mysterious powers governing the universe is not to exact obedience, punish, and destroy but rather to give."

Under the Goddess, in other words, the universe loves us as a mother loves her children. It is infinitely forgiving, infinitely supportive, infinitely kind. Unlike the archetypal "Father," it is not so much about laws and consequences as it is about nurturance.

The cosmos as the breast from which we suck the milk of life: imaged that way, the idea that the sky is inherently meaningful immediately makes sense, whether we are living in the Neolithic period or today. All of us need food to be happy; we need comfort, friends, sexual release, physical safety. "Mother Nature" often provides all that.

But we need more. Happiness is not determined only by the meeting of physical requirements. We also need a sense of purpose, a framework that gives meaning to our individual lives. Under the mythic Goddess, wouldn't it make sense that, along with our need for food and shelter, our spiritual needs would also be met?

If the universe is our loving Mother, won't she know that our hunger is not only in the belly?

Through this line of reasoning, so foreign to our puritanical, punitive Judeo-Christian sensibilities, the Goddess mentality provides an intellectual climate that leads directly to astrological assumptions. *The sky, like the rest of life, cares for us.* The earth brings forth food, the clean air fills our lungs, and the sky gives us meaning and inspiration: food and air for the human spirit.

The amazing point, which Eisler develops most convincingly, is that once we had all that; we danced and made love, lived and died, without shame, under the wing of the generous, living cosmos, imaged as a great Mother.

And then we sold it for *Rambo* spin-offs.

This "intellectual triumph of the Mother civilization" that we call "astrology" did not pop into existence overnight. Some say it only goes back to the early Greeks, but that is really a question mostly of semantics. The broader idea of astrology is patently ancient. Just think of the Pyramids or of Stonehenge and get the idea. Hundreds of thousands of years passed before the edifice we know as astrology today took shape.

Bones, many of them dating back to the Upper Paleolithic twenty or thirty millennia ago, have been found in Ice Age archeological sites. These bones are often marked with a series of crude crosshatches. Until 1965, scholars assumed the marks were decorative, or that perhaps they represented some kind of hunting "kill-count." Then Alexander Marshack, a researcher at the Peabody Museum of Archaeology and Ethnology, took a closer look. The incisions, rough as they are, show a pattern: they appear to be a tally of moon phases. They may very well represent one of humanity's first stabs at recording its experience.

And what were our Ice Age grandmothers and grandfathers recording? The sky—always the mysterious, ominous sky.

I am entertained reading reports of discoveries such as Alexander Marshack's. Often the accounts are dry, written from a narrowly academic perspective. That rigor and precision is commendable, but it can lead to blunders, such as the assumption that these Paleolithic moon-worshippers were coolly "doing science" … a fairly "obvious" conclusion, given that the person drawing it is often a scientist himself or herself. But the conjured image is ludicrous: spectral hunter-gatherers huddle before my eyes, sipping instant coffee from Styrofoam cups, zealously attempting to squeeze the cosmos into a rational, post-Newtonian model … just like the scientist who's doing the conjuring.

Those Mother-worshipping bone-engravers from the Upper Paleolithic: who were they really and what were they up to? Ultimately, we cannot know. But surely, in their view of the sky they must have held more in common with the magical-meaningful spirit of astrology than with the dispassionate observations of modern astronomy. In the framework of a culture in which the cosmos was imaged as the Great Goddess, by watching the moon, our forebears expected to find more than practical information. They expected spiritual sustenance too.

By reflex, we may immediately groan, shoving that Paleolithic expectation into the category of superstition. We may think of it as "quaint," certainly as "primitive." But let's use a different word. Not primitive, but primal. And let's remember, with C. J. Cherryh, that "even to believe we can't know the universe is a system."

Maybe those Goddess-worshipping hunter-gatherers understood something that we have forgotten. The Gauquelins' data suggest so, as does an open-minded consideration of the sunspot cycle. The long list of acute observers who accepted astrology suggests the same.

And maybe "forgotten" is not actually the right word. Maybe astrology, and the Goddess, and women, and gentle men, and the left hand … maybe all of them have been victims of something darker than a lapse of memory.

Maybe they have been mugged, taken and bound in a cellar—and maybe they will emerge again together.

Ultimately of course the only question that matters for our purposes is, does astrology work? We can study the Gauquelins' results. We can consider the sunspot cycle. And, if we please, we can try imagining the universe as the Great Mother. But, finally, it comes down to individuals. Can astrology make your own life more comprehensible, more meaningful, happier? Is it real for you?

Naturally, no book can answer that question. But those who fear astrology would encourage you not even to ask it. They would rule by authority and by ridicule. They would characterize my astrological colleagues and myself as tricksters, and you—if you sat with us—as a gullible fool.

And they would do all that in the name of science, reason and common sense. That is *Astrophobia*.

A couple of weeks ago, I did an astrological reading for an artist. As such work goes, it was routine, the stuff of my daily life for the last fifteen years. I wove images and tales, trying to capture the journey I saw mirrored in her birthchart. The woman herself is articulate and alert. Given her nature, social standing and education, she would certainly be taken seriously in any court of law.

A few days later, I received a note from her. Here is what she wrote: "I've listened to the tapes all the way through three times and I feel I've just begun to assimilate what you said. I've been on an incredible high since Monday … to be mirrored in such a way is profoundly affirming … the separate elements were not totally new—and yet the overall picture was shocking … inspiring, challenging, comforting … It was a gift … one of the most important of my life."

A fool, my victim … or one upon whom the Goddess has rained grace?

5

SPARKS

One day, seven million years ago, a photon flashed silently from the heart of a galaxy. One night, seven million years later, it reached its destination: the retina of my right eye. I was standing at the eyepiece of a telescope, bundled against the Piscean winter chill. In the circle of my sight, an image of ghostly loveliness slowly emerged. I breathed gently, willing my pupil to dilate even further, welcoming the pale, ancient light.

Minutes passed. Still I waited. The patience of seven-million-year-old light is contagious. Often in my galaxy-gazing, I've felt as though I were a wrinkled Japanese gardener, serenely pruning an evergreen bough, needle by needle.

My left eye saw nothing; it was tightly closed. In my right eye, a distant star-hive glowed as though it were winter breath under a street lamp. Lens-shaped, mottled with dust-clouds, the faint image belied the creature's gargantuan vital statistics. The galaxy appeared tiny and gossamer light, as though a puff of wind could blow it away.

One of my first memories as a little boy was wanting a telescope for Christmas. I was given one, but I was disappointed. I expected Mount Palomar. I got a spyglass. Still, within a few years I began an active pursuit of amateur astronomy, climbing to the roof of the New York apartment building where my family lived on almost every clear night, trying to get a glimpse of whatever was on the other side of the crap they had pumped into the atmosphere that day. The lurid yellow haze, nearly incandescent from Manhattan's glare, made it tough to see much of anything.

But there was another veil to penetrate, as opaque as brick: my own expectations. I had read authoritative astronomy books. I subscribed to *Sky and Telescope* magazine. I often pored over astrophysics in lieu of doing my homework.

I thought I knew what galaxies were.

Now, thirty years later, I am not so sure. My telescope is bigger and my skies are darker, clearer. My heart too: darker, clearer. I am more suspicious of the answers each Age sells its children.

Staring at that spindly, pale image in the eyepiece, my mind was unconcerned with the mass of technicalities that we so often mistake for real knowing. I forgot that we labeled this ghost "Messier 82." I didn't care that it was seven million light-years away and bound gravitationally to Messier 91. That its light was polarized, that it emitted radio frequencies, even that it appeared to have undergone some manner of cataclysm—none of that mattered to me then. I was struck by something else, something so intuitively evident and unmistakable that I could not imagine ever having been blind enough to miss it.

The galaxy was alive.

Once, while cruising in my old trimaran, *Nimble Hope*, near Beaufort, North Carolina, a huge dolphin suddenly emerged beside me not three feet from where I sat steering. For a few seconds we considered each other, then the dolphin slipped beneath the waves. I will always remember that strange, eloquent eye. It conveyed so much: consciousness, intelligence, individuality. But above all, alienness. Here was a creature with a quality akin to wisdom, something that evokes the word "soul." And yet that wisdom was impenetrable. I could witness it ... I could not help but witness it. But I could never understand it.

It was the same with my galaxy. That enigmatic, perhaps even indefinable quality we call "life" coursed through it.

How could I tell? The answer, naturally, transcends logic. It is something left-handed, something of the Goddess, something trans-rational. Life resonates with life. Why do we sense it when someone tiptoes into our darkened bedroom? Why do we "feel someone's eyes on us?" Why do plants grow more vigorously when we love them? Who knows? But one thing I do know: whatever animates me, whatever mysterious quantity makes me alive, I recognized it mirrored in that cloud of distant stars.

A living galaxy. Intelligent. Aware. Even emotional, perhaps. At first glance, the proposition seems ludicrous, counter to common sense. But common sense, as Albert Einstein once observed, is basically whatever we are taught to believe before we are nineteen years old. None of us, at least for a very long time, has been given any encouragement to imagine that the universe itself is alive. Yet consider: a cell contains approximately ten billion atoms. A human brain is composed of about ten billion cells. Ten billion stars is a reasonable estimate for the population of an average galaxy—most of them are much smaller than our Milky Way. Is some principle in operation here that our cultural blinders prevent us from seeing? Why is it "common sense" to assume that intelligence and life can only exist within a matrix of tissue?

One of the thorniest problems in modern astrophysics lies in determining the ultimate fate of the universe. Maybe it will expand indefinitely until the cosmos is nothing but an unimaginably thin veil of cool cinders. That is what cosmologists call the "open universe." Alternatively, the current expansion may eventually give way to an equally languorous contraction—the "closed universe."

No one knows which model is right, although current theory leans toward infinite expansion.

Hidden in the question is another riddle, even more profound. Why does the universe exist at all? This is not strictly a metaphysical mystery, even though it will quickly bring us back to the question of an intelligence implicit in the universe. If the initial mass of the cosmos were even slightly greater, the universe would have collapsed in on itself long before galaxies, let alone biological life, evolved. If, on the other hand, the universe had been even slightly *less* massive, it would have blown away like perfume in a hurricane.

Stephen Hawking is perhaps the greatest theoretical physicist of our era. In his view, "a universe like ours with galaxies and stars is actually quite unlikely. If one considers the possible constants and laws that could have emerged, the odds against a universe that has produced life like ours are immense."

In other words, according to current cultural models, the existence of life is not a very scientific notion. Hawking again: "The most remarkable thing about the universe is that it is so close to the borderline between open and closed. The probabilities against it being on such a borderline arc enormous ..." Significantly, he adds, "I think there are clearly religious implications whenever you start to discuss the origins of the universe."

For most of us, this is abstruse material, certainly not the kind of thinking one expects to find in a book about astrology. Yet my premise is that the inherent meaningfulness of the universe is quite consistent with implications of modern cosmology. Or to put it more bluntly, the universe offers us some pretty good evidence that it is intelligent and purposeful. To me, those words imply something very close to the word "alive."

The notion that the cosmos itself is a conscious being is heretical today. It was not always so controversial. In *Timaeus*, Plato writes, "Now when the Creator had framed the soul according to his will, he formed within her the corporeal universe, and brought the two together, and united them center to center ... The body of heaven is visible, but the soul is invisible, and partakes of reason ..."

In the fourth century BC, people had no telescopes. But they had eyes, and the night, and hearts with different instincts than our own. Was Plato wrong? Our technology is certainly superior, but that is not really relevant. Technologically, it may be correct to describe a human being as a mass of cells composed primarily of carbon, oxygen, and hydrogen. But in putting it that way, we obviously miss something significant, something instruments and measuring devices cannot capture.

Often in high school astronomy classes, a teacher will dismiss astrology by observing that since the ancients could not explain what the planets really were, they imagined them to be living creatures—gods and goddesses. Certainly in most early cultures, the sun, moon, and planets bore the names of deities and were associated with them. Is this superstition? Or is it a powerful and not-so-unrealistic metaphor that we may still be able to unravel, and thereby recover an elemental truth about our place in the universe?

SKY GODS

The planets are gods! How out of place those words sound today. Yet if the cosmos itself is alive, then all its parts are somehow part of the process of life. Do the planets somehow mediate between us and the unfathomable living mystery of deep space? Are they intercessors? Certainly, a goatherd in Plato's time might not have thought in those terms. To him or her, life was simpler: the planets, like the gods, "did things" to one, arbitrarily and incomprehensibly. The fact that these "things" could sometimes be anticipated by watching the motions of Jupiter or Mercury offered a sliver of comfort. The good news was that the planet-gods, like ourselves, could perhaps be manipulated through appeals to their vanity, or through fervent supplications rendered more plausible through financial sacrifices ... a scene not terribly different from what we often observe in modern churches.

But did Plato think that way? Was he as naïve as that high school astronomy teacher would have us imagine? Here are his own words, again from *Timaeus*: "God … gave us sight to the end that we might behold the courses of intelligence in the heaven, and apply them to the courses of our own intelligence, which are akin to them …"

"The courses of intelligence in the heaven." An awkward phrase, as it should be. If it were smoother on the tongue, we might not linger with it. Plato is saying something radical here, something so foreign to our modern mind-sets that we might well miss it entirely. "And our own intelligence which are akin to them." Again, an alien notion, nearly lost in the gnarling mists that separate cultures and ages.

Of what does Plato speak? Kinship, linkage: human consciousness bonded to yet another consciousness, larger, all-embracing … yet located not in the abstract, positionless "Heaven" of modern theology, but rather in that older, more concrete "heaven," the literal, physical sky. That is Plato's astrology, vastly more sophisticated than the goatherd's. The sky to him is symbolic. But more than that: the sky is intelligent. Its "symbolism" is closer in tone to a human gesture than to a wooden crucifix. It is a conscious signal, not a static sign. And it is not obscure or even very mysterious: we can read it easily because our own intelligence is "akin" to the "intelligence in the heaven."

Astrology is an elaborate, technical system. Learning all its ins and outs is a serious undertaking requiring many years of study. All kinds of people attend astrological conventions, from all over the social, psychological and philosophical spectrums. Yet in my experience, one trait runs true among virtually all the teachers and the majority of the attendees: fine, sharp intellects.

Still, the heart of astrology is simple: one looks at the sky, engages imagination and emotion, then reads the heavens as though they were a poem. It is easy, almost reflexive. Why? Because, as Plato says, our intelligences are akin to the intelligence of the sky. We speak the same language.

Watch:

Sunlight cheers us, energizes us, makes us feel alive. Its astrological meaning? Vitality. The life force. The juice that makes us want to get out of bed in the morning. The sun is the gravitational center of the solar system. It holds everything together. Similarly, there is something inside you that holds you together, gives you identity, unites your paradoxes well enough for you to function as an individual. That is the sun.

The moon? Just let your mind free-associate. Moon: night, feelings, magic, tears, romance, seeing ghosts, having a dream … And that too is solid, familiar astrology: the lunar side of the human psyche equates with our subjective processes. It is the *mood* of life, our instincts, our feelings.

Mercury buzzes around the sky faster than any other planet. It resonates with the busiest, fastest "circuit" in human consciousness: our thoughts, our speech and our senses.

Venus is the brightest and whitest of the planets. Because it is never far from the setting or rising sun, typically, one observes it shining brilliantly in the deep blue twilight of sunset or dawn, a diamond set in azure. Its meaning? The goddess of beauty, of balance, and of love.

The "intelligence in the heaven" was succinct with Mars, the traditional war-god. She painted him the color of blood. Astrologically, Mars represents conflict, but also courage and the force of the will.

Jupiter is the largest planet by far, hosting a retinue of four world-sized moons. Even a quick glimpse of the "king of the gods" through a telescope reveals a strikingly oblate disk. Jupiter appears to be overweight, bloated about the middle. Consistently, the planet signifies bigness and plenty. It represents a warmhearted, big-spirited, generous part of the human psyche, but one which may overextend or overindulge.

Saturn's motion is by far the slowest of any of the classical planets. It refers to plodding and difficulty … and to the virtues they engender: self-discipline, patience, and persistence.

These were all the planets the ancients knew. But in 1781, William Herschel discovered Uranus. It gets a little more complicated with the "discovered" planets, but the same pattern holds: their meaning can be accurately deduced from intuitive, poetic observation. But with these new planets, we have a second family of hints. Their meanings are bound synchronistically to the tenor of the times in which they were discovered.

Curiously, the planet Uranus is actually bright enough to be seen with the unaided eye. Knowing where to look, I have observed it without difficulty even through damp, light-polluted East Coast skies. Given the elaborate visual astronomy of the Egyptian, Babylonian, Chinese, and Meso-American cultures, I find it remarkable that Uranus waited so long to be found. More about that riddle in a few seconds …

What is the meaning of Uranus? Here is one line of reasoning: what is north for Earth is north, more or less, for all the other planets. The effect is that as planets orbit the sun, they spin on their axes. It works for all the planets except Uranus, whose rotational axis is pointed more-or-less toward the sun. So Uranus *rolls where other planets spin.* That is a relatively recent astronomical discovery, but in a sense, astrologers anticipated it: they discovered that when Uranus is prominent in a person's birthchart, he or she tends to "hear a different drummer," to individuate colorfully, to be in some sense a rebel. The person, in other words, "rolls where others spin."

Significantly, Uranus made its historical debut between the American and French revolutions, a time when distinctly Uranian virtues of self-determination and independence were sweeping through the collective mind. It appears that we were only able to see the planet in the sky when, as a culture, we were ready to "see" it within ourselves. A strange, unsettling idea, but consistent with the mysteries we are exploring.

Neptune, the Lord of the Sea, is the last of the major planets, standing on the edge of the abyss of space, and representing the antithesis of the solar ego: mysticism, trance, self-transcendence, compassion. It was discovered in 1846. As I wrote in *The Inner Sky*, "In the decades immediately following Neptune's discovery, Neptunian values and preoccupations swept through humanity like a storm. The Romantic movement in the arts. The rise of spiritualism – séances and mesmerism. The inception of mystical organizations, like the Theosophical Society. The arrival of the first wave of Hindu and Buddhist teachers in the West as the British Empire linked Europe to India … As a species, humanity was ready to discover Neptune."

One more word remains in the planet-poem, so far as we now know: Pluto. The last of the planets is tiny. Most of the time, it is nearly invisible, swinging out beyond Neptune into the dim, icy emptiness beyond the pale of the sun. Every couple of centuries, Pluto cuts inward, coming closer to us than Neptune, carrying messages from the darkness. There's the poetic key: messages from the dark—our deepest fears and taboos, the shame with which we have been touched. All this often-unconscious material is Plutonian territory. Evil, and the capacity to resist it, is too. It is no accident that Pluto's 1930 discovery prefigured an incomprehensible outburst of fascist sadism.

Together, the planets form an elaborate and subtle model of the human mind. Each one resonates with some aspect of our humanity. Each, like the gods and goddesses whose names they bear, has wisdom and blindness, riches and poverty. Each has lessons to teach and warnings to deliver. All ten function in everyone, but in different tones and balances, depending upon their actual configuration in the person's birthchart.

And they work.

Several of my clients have doctorates in psychology. One, a Taurean woman who specializes in working with sexually abused children, told me, "One of the things that challenged me was that in that initial reading you gave me as much information about myself that was useful and practical as I could give someone in a psychological evaluation."

She also told me she first came to see me out of curiosity, half expecting the experience to be "hokey." Yet the planets spoke to her, just as they did to the seminal astronomer-astrologer Johannes Kepler, born in 1571. He wrote, "A most unfailing experience (as far as it can be expected in nature) of the excitement of sublunary natures by the conjunctions and aspects of the planets has instructed and compelled my unwilling belief."

If the mind is open, the sky speaks.

Books are written about each one of these psycho-planetary bodies, and the books themselves only scratch the surface. The thumbnail sketches I have provided here are consistent with astrological tradition and practice, but they are necessarily abbreviated. My aim has not been so much to offer an introduction to planetary symbolism as to show how simple and obvious that symbolism can be.

The Goddess-Universe is not testing us: She is helping us. And Her message, once we make peace with the medium, is clearer than any human speech.

But the planets are only part of that message. Behind them, beyond them, is another signal, another gift, far more portentous. It is our Rosetta stone, the key that unlocks the sky. Let's consider it.

6

SKY

Once I heard a Muskogee elder speak. He told us about how he had been invited to address an astrological conference. He had tried to get the conferees interested in going outside under the night sky. No one wanted to go. *They were afraid they might get mosquito bites.*

The story was barbed, and told with irony. To me, it was very sad. Too often we astrologers, immersed in our books and our computer programs, fail to consult that ultimate source of astrological knowledge: the sky itself. And that oversight drains our work of life and magic, pushing it toward a barren landscape of cold academic theory.

So put on your bug repellent and follow me out through the garden, down the path, across the meadow … into the night. We've brought a blanket. Spread it out, lie down and let your eyes slowly open. The Milky Way is soaring overhead, glowing like a vast ghost. Stars are burning, blue and red and pale yellow.

Relax. Take it in. Let an hour pass. Amazing what we forget: we are all creatures in a galaxy, little intelligences lost in space. Funny how people long for starships when the reality is that we were born on one and we will die on one.

What is out there in the cosmos as you gaze up at it? What do you actually see? And forget astronomy, forget the latest version of the Ultimate Truth. What does the universe look like directly to your senses?

Like vast, dark space. Infinite. Mysterious. Speckled with sharp points of light, and eerie glows.

Now, still lying flat on your back, close your eyes. Shut out the sky. What do you see now with your eyes shut tight?

Another universe, one we call the mind.

And how does that inner universe appear?

Familiar ground: like vast, dark space. Infinite. Mysterious. Speckled with sharp points of light and eerie glows.

Mind and sky: how similar they are when we engage our innocent, untutored senses, how alike they feel. Theories and preconceptions set aside, innocence and simplicity arise. Good teachers, sometimes. Instantly, the primal perception upon which astrology rests emerges: *mind and sky are one.* Each is built around the same laws and principles, and each one feels about the same to that elusive nerve-ending we call our awareness.

Astrologically, the formula is traditionally expressed this way: "As above, so below." We can learn about the structure of the mind by considering the sky.

And it works backwards too: we can learn about the sky by considering the mind.

The first notion—that the planets give us insight into personality—is the core of practical astrology. We observe swift Mercury resonating with the lightning flash of our thoughts, the changeable moon reflecting the seasons of our changeable hearts, and so on. But consider the second notion: that we can learn about the sky by watching the mind. This idea is like a trail of bread crumbs: follow it far enough and you'll come face to face with a witch. Or a Goddess.

Again, close your eyes. Call it meditation if you want. Or call it something else. No matter, just open yourself to what is always there inside you, behind all your opinions and personal history. What is the most basic statement you can make about what you find? Maybe this: that you are alive, that there is something conscious inside you.

Now apply our formula: as below, so above. Again, it works both ways. The conclusion: awareness within yourself equals or implies some kind of awareness that lies beyond yourself.

As you are conscious, so is the cosmos.

Once again, we find ourselves seeing through Plato's eyes, acknowledging "the intelligence in the Heaven," reflecting our own. And this time the evidence is woven into the structure of our minds, more intimate than breath.

Apollo 14 astronaut Edgar Mitchell spoke (*New Age Journal*, March/April 1990) of the unexpected impact of his unique view of the heavens: "What happened to me was that, as I looked at Earth and saw the cosmos, saw the universe, laid out before me, with this tiny little planet and these millions and billions of stars and galaxies and galactic clusters ... I had the irrefutable feeling within myself that this is an intelligent system I'm looking at. That it is not, as we in science had characterized it, a random collection made from the random collisions of energy-matter.

That there is a coherence, that there is an intelligence palpable in the universe."

Back to the meadow, back to the stars. An astronaut voyaging to the moon has a better view, but under clear, dark skies our own perspective is not so terribly different from Edgar Mitchell's. Our eyes can see almost the same thing that he saw. Can our minds and hearts see what he saw too?

Gaze at the sky, and soon the heart fills with an exquisite longing. Silly maybe to put words on it: "we long for God," or for Peace, for Oneness, for Heaven … take your pick. Words are important sometimes. Not here, not now. I'm writing and you're reading, but I am trying to speak to a part of you that cruises deeper than language.

Simple truth: the core of your being *wants something*. It is full of longing

… a hungry longing that is perhaps the most basic quality of human awareness. Mystics tell us that it is ultimately an urge "to return to the Source." More words—maybe the best ones we will ever find. But certainly that inner hunger is mutable, subject to distortions. People translate it, imagining that they'll find that elusive bliss if only they hit the lottery, if only they make love to this person or that person, if only they find the money for another drink … But the appetite is never satisfied. The hunger remains.

Deep water. I won't trivialize the human condition by offering up any more "answers." We already have plenty of them, and a fat lot of good they do us. My point is a little different. Again we apply our formula, "as below, so above." *That longing we feel must also be inherent to the structure of the cosmos.* As we hunger for oneness with the universe, so does the cosmos long for us.

The Goddess is calling.

Or name it God. Or Divinity. Or Jesus. Or the Dharmakaya. You know the list.

THE FAILURE OF ASTROLOGY

The Astronomical Society of the Pacific is a spiritual cousin to the infamous CSICOP, just as eager to declare astrology a capital heresy contrary to the Holy Writ of Newtonian Science. They publish a booklet called *Astrology and Astronomy* which they advertise in one of the astronomical journals to which I subscribe. I held my nose and sent them four bucks. What I got was a collection of photocopied newspaper articles "debunking" astrology. The articles summarize various scientific, statistical studies that indicate the ineffectiveness of Sun Signs in predicting much of anything. Here's an example:

"Bernie Silverman, a psychologist at Michigan State University, asked astrologers to predict which astrological signs would be compatible and incompatible according to their horoscopes. He then obtained records for 2,978 couples who got married and 478 couples who got divorced in Michigan in 1967 and 1968. When he looked at their birthdays and signs, he found no correlation with the predictions of the astrologers. Compatible signs got married—and divorced—just as often as incompatible ones."

Here's another:

"John McGervey, a physicist at Case Western Reserve University, looked up the birthdays of the 16,634 scientists listed in *American Men of Science* and of the

6,475 politicians listed in *Who's Who in American Politics.* Certainly you might expect that scientists and politicians (two decidedly non-average groups) would tend to cluster more among certain signs of the zodiac —and certain personality types—than others. Yet McGervey found no such tendency."

Naturally, given the political bias of *Astrology and Astronomy*, no studies are quoted in which anything like a positive astrological effect is noted. The Gauquelins' work regarding the planetary correlation with career is conspicuous in its absence. In fact, the only mention of the Gauquelins is a single reference to a study they did regarding possible hereditary astrological effects linking parents and their children. The article states, "Gauquelin's results, however, were completely negative: Astrological factors are not hereditary."

Contrast that assertion with the words of Michel Gauquelin himself, taken from his book, *Birthtimes:* "The results, published in 1966 in my book, *L'Hérédité Planétaire*, showed up the effect of a planetary similarity between parents and children ... Eleven years later, this planetary heredity was confirmed by myself and my collaborators after a second investigation into more than 30,000 birth dates of parents and children ..." He adds, "In the 'absurd' field of planetary heredity, you can never prove too much and, thanks to this collection of over 60,000 births, I was in a position to describe fairly precisely what I called 'the planetary effect on heredity.'"

The Gauquelins' hereditary results are "completely negative"? Did the author writing for the Astronomical Society of the Pacific even read their work?

Still, truth said, the Astronomical Society of the Pacific does quote serious studies in which astrology fails. The two investigations described a few paragraphs back are flawed by their focus on Sun Signs alone. But astrology has flunked other more elaborate tests. Astrologers have proven unable to link birthcharts correctly with biographies and personality profiles. People misidentified analyses of their own birthcharts in random groups.

The truth, it seems, is that when astrology is subjected to statistical scrutiny, sometimes it passes, sometimes it doesn't. Each side of the debate tends, of course, to publish only that research which is consistent with the "religion" it represents.

For what it is worth, I have a list of thirty-one Sun Sign studies, which I obtained from Mary Ellen Glass, the banned astrology teacher from Towson University about whom I wrote in Chapter Three. In seventeen of the studies, significant astrological effects were noted. Two studies were ambiguous. In twelve, astrology seemed ineffective.

What should we believe?

Let's return to our meadow and our fields of starlight, far from the harsh fluorescent bulbs of "objectivity." Let's listen to the Muskogee elder, slip out into the sacred darkness and let the night speak.

Consciousness within us, consciousness beyond us. As we know the living universe, so does the "Intelligence in the Heaven" know us. As we long for something we cannot define, that same mystery longs for us. We are on a journey; the night is our road. Or a metaphor for our road.

Confusing, going back and forth like this between science and poetry ... but are we not all poets and scientists? Are we not all capable of reason and also of something beyond reason? Can there ever be a satisfying answer to life's most elemental questions which does not speak to both sides of our humanity?

Astrology fails sometimes; that is a fact. It succeeds sometimes too. The rational parts of our minds are bewildered. Perhaps we are tempted to take refuge in prejudice and preconception. But bring in the heart: it reminds us of something both dogmatic scientists and dogmatic astrologers often forget. We are on a mysterious journey and no one will be the same when it is over. Life changes us, and that elasticity makes us very tough creatures to measure.

And that is really my main point. As we distill the philosophical basis of astrology down to its essential elixir, we must recognize simply that we are all moving targets. We change and we grow. The implications of this for astrological research are enormous.

CATERPILLARS?

You've seen them—crawly little boogers with a zillion legs. But catch them a few weeks earlier: They are tiny crystalline eggs embedded in the bark of a tree. Or a few weeks later … they are now balls of silken thread hanging from a branch. Then butterflies. Then dust.

What can we really say about a caterpillar? Can the creature be defined at all?

You are like that. Me too. Once I was shy. Now I am pretty comfortable winging a talk before a big audience. "Steven Forrest is an introvert." Bullseye in 1965. Questionable in 1992. What about in 2020? Who knows? Yet I am a Capricorn throughout my life, so if "being a Capricorn" is going to mean anything, it had better mean something flexible.

That simple, obvious idea—that life is change—is the key that unlocks all the paradoxes. Most scientific studies of astrology have started from the premise that the signs and planets must "mean something." Specifically, that implies that they must mean something rigid and readily definable, something that can be defined and then measured.

This in my opinion is a fundamental error. I do not blame astrology's critics for it. Astrologers themselves have often perpetuated the mistake. But imagine that we set out to investigate the proposition that caterpillars are squiggly things with lots of legs. We will prove it conclusively one week, then disprove it just as conclusively the next.

Which is a fine description of what has occurred in the realm of statistical investigations of astrology.

Rob Hand, a well-known astrologer and one of the most intelligent people I have ever met, once quipped, "Personality is the modern word for fate." Medieval astrological texts are full of dark pronouncements such as "the native is beset by secret enemies and wasting diseases." Much of it was fatalistic stuff. By and large, the astrologers of that period were not greatly concerned with character, and even less with what we might call psychology. They wanted to know "what would happen."

We modern practitioners often imagine that we have gone far beyond those grim cubbyholes, but often we have simply traded one dungeon for another. We used to be trapped in our "fates." Now, too often, we're trapped in our "personalities" at least according to pop astrology.

But let's not forget astrology's mystical heart, nor compartmentalize it away from the attempt to make an objective, rational evaluation of the system. There is a fire, a drive, deep in the core of every living being, something that gets us out of bed in the morning, then propels us through a thousand changes. That is not just abstract philosophy. That means that you are constantly changing. Your chart is more verb than noun. The notion that Capricorn people are shy is not "simply wrong sometimes."

The error is far more fundamental than that—just as misleading as saying "once a caterpillar, always a caterpillar."

The birthchart, astrology's basic tool, is literally a map. Superficially, it shows the heavens as they appeared when we drew our first breath. But deeply, the birthchart also maps our road back to the sky. It shows the *way of the hunger*, and points toward where it is leading us.

Fate and personality are static words. If life is a journey, then we must reject them. People change. Their charts do not. And logic dictates that all attempts to "pin down" individual characteristics, linking them in deterministic fashion to celestial configurations, must return flawed and ambiguous results.

Bottom line, when we mis-define astrology that way and then test our erroneous definition, we observe "seventeen studies" in which "significant astrological effects were noted, two with ambiguous results, and twelve in which astrology seemed ineffective."

Translation: seventeen times it was a caterpillar, twelve times it was not—and twice it was something indeterminate.

TRIGGERS

The meta logic of astrology must in the end be called "mystical," but that is not to say there are no concretely useful stops along the way. Astrological symbolism is employed successfully in planning businesses, and in forecasting everything from earthquakes to economic cycles to fashion trends. Astrology even does a reasonable job as a "personality inventory."

But, in the final analysis, the birthchart speaks of our need to experience something that is very difficult to describe in earthly language. Here we seem to be in the position of three-dimensional creatures trying to encompass a four-dimensional concept. Call it enlightenment, heaven, union with the divine … we offer up the words to the Night, and they don't even echo once.

So what do we really have in a birthchart—or a life, for that matter? Hunger, a journey, and a map. The rest is speculation or vanity.

So let's take a closer look at the map.

Beyond the planets themselves, basic to astrology are the twelve signs and twelve houses. Why twelve? Why not ten or a hundred? In the next couple of chapters, we'll try to unravel that question. Suffice it now to say that at the most elemental level, the astrological map implies that there are a dozen fundamental modalities of consciousness and experience, and that each one is potentially a path back to "the Goddess" or to some higher state of being.

An investigation of these twelve evolutionary roads quickly reveals one intriguing fact: most of them involve *activity*. Things we do. Working. Traveling. Building relationships. Only a few center exclusively on the interior life. Specifically, of the twelve sign/house concepts, nine are rooted in outward experience and three on the inner realms. We will explore all twelve in detail in Chapter Nine, but now we are just flying over the astrological landscape at a hundred thousand feet, snapping pictures.

What do we see?

Twelve journeys. Nine outward, three inward. The Goddess/Cosmos is telling us something here, something that violates a central precept of many spiritual traditions: that the bulk of our evolutionary experience has more to do with living than with sitting alone in meditation. To be alive, to follow one's human heart, to trust the impulses of the wise monkey we all carry beneath our skin: that is three-quarters of our spiritual work. The "Intelligence in the Heaven" loves us; the cosmos was not made to ensnare or deceive us, but rather to help us,

How?

Here's the key: for every one of us individually, there are certain elemental experiences which seem effective at triggering insight and realization. Having kids. Taking religious vows. Getting married. Studying quantum physics. Not all of them can be packed into a single biography. There is not enough time. More importantly, the personal characteristics that enable someone to prosper in a monastic environment may not assist him or her in facing the noisy indignities of child-rearing.

So, for each individual we can imagine an optimal path through life, one which best fills that person with enthusiasm and verve. Your path and mine may differ; they probably do. But they hold one critical point in common: if we follow them, we will be glad we're alive.

Your astrological chart, at its heart, simply maps the right path for you. It is more akin to a suggestion than to a prediction. It does not "tell you who you are." It cannot do that, because evolutionary astrology ultimately rejects the myth of some static, immobile, immutable Self. Instead, it speaks of a journey. A journey that changes you.

In the best of all possible worlds, astrology would be quite unnecessary. We would all be raised by perfect parents, loved unconditionally, guided faultlessly, encouraged to be whoever we naturally were. We would then follow our profoundest impulses, creating outer biographies which unerringly matched the contours of our spirits.

But life is trickier than that. Thirty-some years ago, I sat in front of the television, watching *Superman*. I had my eye on old George Reeves, with his cape and his glinting eyes. I was thinking, "He's a big white guy … I'm a little white guy …" I began to get a sense of what would soon be expected of me.

And you ladies of my generation: you were watching the Man of Steel rescue the plucky but hapless Lois Lane, and coming to parallel conclusions.

We were poisoned, as all generations are poisoned. Over the core of our beings there was grafted a set of myths and assumptions which make it awfully difficult for us to hear those inner promptings of true individuality. Distortions; neuroses; psychic constraints: the downside of civilization. God help me, I was thirty-two and going through a divorce before I recovered enough of myself even to be able to cry.

Did my birthchart rescue me? Of course not. But it helped. It told me I'm a Capricorn, and that an "occupational hazard" associated with that sign is a constriction of emotional expression—the price I pay for my ability to work really hard. It told me of my "spy's moon" in the hidden Fourth House, and of how easily I become the invisible man. It told me of my Scorpio south node, and of how the hardest, most important lesson I face in this life has to do with relaxing control and trusting the soul of the moment.

The chart went further: it outlined my current circumstances in spooky detail, and advised me about alternative courses, some wiser, some not so wise. It spoke in language that might seem initially obscure—secondary progressed Moon in Gemini in the Seventh House, Uranus transiting the Ascendant—but it is a language anyone can learn. In fact, once you have sat with the planets for a while, you begin to realize that astrology is the fundamental language with which your brain is programmed. Deep down, you have known it for a long, long time.

The sky is the extended hand of the Great Mother. In her fingers, we find a gift of planets, little speckles of light against the crow-black vastness. Read them and they'll make you shiver, as though you were looking the ancient Goddess straight in the eye.

They tell you why you were born.

They speak to you of a road, strangely familiar even though you have not yet traveled it, that leads to a foreign land for which you have longed since time began.

They remind you of your heart and of the wisdom of trusting it.

They tell you how to be human.

7

THE ARGUMENT OF COLOR

Unless you are a blind person and someone is reading this book to you, there is color all around you. It may be the gray walls of a prison or the blue of a wide open April sky. But color is there. It is omnipresent. Even in pitch dark, even in dreams, the images that dance through the mind are charged with blooms and blushes of every tint.

Aesthetically, one of the glories of color lies in its infinite diversity. There are so many hues and shades. Storm clouds are gray; so is slate; so might be your lover's eyes. Each has a different beauty, and a different depth.

But the apparent infinite diversity of color masks a simpler reality lying just beneath the surface. The colors of the world follow a few elemental laws.

As we will see, they are the same laws that underlie astrology.

Back in kindergarten, you learned that there are three *primary colors*: red, yellow, and blue. What that means, without getting into a physics lecture, is pretty straight-forward. If you were an artist stuck on a desert island with three tubes of paint—red, yellow, and blue—you might be seriously inconvenienced, but you would have all the paint you would ever need. By mixing them, you could create any color the eye can see. That's why they're called "primary."

Mix red with yellow. You get orange. Yellow with blue; green appears. Blend red and blue: instant violet.

You have six colors now: three primaries, three *secondaries*. And of course you could "mix the mixes" once more, producing the standard color wheel known to all students of art, design, or physics. How many colors do you see now?

Twelve—a familiar number. The color wheel, as it is commonly represented, looks quite a lot like the ancient zodiac.

We can of course easily "mix the mixes" yet again and make twenty-four colors, or forty-eight, or ninety-six. These are numbers that have no obvious astrological significance. And when we mix red with yellow, we can emphasize the red a little bit, producing orange again, but with a deeper, warmer tone.

Quickly, something approaching an infinity of shades can be generated, which is what we actually see in nature and every department store.

So does color really have any connection with astrology? If in fact we can produce an endless array of shades, what's so special about the number twelve? Let's go back to our desert island—but now let's treat our stranded artist more harshly. Let's take away just one of her three original tubes of paint, leaving her with only two … any two. Like Picasso in his "blue period," she might still be able to paint a masterpiece, but she'll be working under a dreadful restraint: two-thirds of the colors that delight our eyes would be missing from her canvases.

We are looking at something truly primal here: the palette of the world that strikes our optic nerves can he built from three colors. No more are needed, but no fewer will do. At some ancient, interior level, our brains are adapted to these parameters. And as the three primaries brew the infinite palette of nature, behind the mesmerizing chaos, there lies a simple progression: three colors, six colors, twelve colors ...

And behind the mesmerizing chaos of astrological symbolism, we see exactly the same progression. Three signs lying equidistant from each other in the zodiac are said to be "fiery." Like the three primary colors, equidistant around the color wheel, the three fire signs link together harmoniously. Artists and decorators speak of the "Triad of Harmony" linking red, yellow, and blue. Astrologers speak of the "trine aspect" peacefully bonding Aries to Leo and Sagittarius,

'The "air" signs, Gemini, Libra, and Aquarius, form a similar harmonious triangle, and correspond to the secondary colors, orange, green, and violet. The "earth" and "water" signs are connected in the same triangular, harmonious way.

The zodiac and the color wheel are both pies with twelve slices. That's a significant parallel—but it is only the beginning. As we begin to discern the inner logic of each circle, the correspondences become more striking. Both systems—the zodiac and the color wheel—are built around *triad*s. In each one, the members of the triads are harmonious. In each the members of the triads form the points of an equilateral triangle.

Opposite shades on the color wheel are called *complementary*. Technically, this is because they share no hues in common. Yellow contains no violet: green contains not a whit of red. Visually, this quality of oppositeness is pleasing; the colors seem to "like" each other.

Again, astrological symbolism parallels the color wheel: Opposite signs are traditionally seen as drawn to each other in an "opposites attract" kind of way. Why? *Because each contains something the other one lacks!* Diplomatic, empathetic Libra is drawn to the forceful, straightforward mood of Aries. Logical, practical Capricorn is complemented by the tenderness of Cancer. Like orange and blue, they have nothing in common, and yet curiously seem to bring out the best in each other. Thus, romantic folklore suggesting that "opposites attract" has an astrological basis—and a basis in the color wheel too.

Once more, the internal logic of each system appears to be the same.

Are these parallels between color theory and the zodiac products of chance? That seems dubious; the correlations are too perfect. Then was astrology simply built around the color wheel in order to lend it credence? That argument fails too; the scientific study of color is a relatively new phenomenon. There is no evidence that the people who gave us the twelve signs had ever heard of the color wheel.

Clinching the last point is a simple, if embarrassing, fact: astrology books are a complete muddle when it comes to assigning colors to signs. Apart from some consistency in linking Aries to red, there is a comical degree of disagreement among the various authorities—as though astrologers themselves have been largely unaware of the systematic, physical ties between their art and the way the optical part of our brains encodes its image of the world.

Astrology did not derive from the color wheel. Better said, *they both seem to reflect some larger, transcendent principle which unifies them.*

Signs are only one piece of astrological symbolism. What about the physical components of the solar system? Does the way we perceive color bear any relationship to the planets?

Long before humanity began to record its memories, our forebears began watching the lights in the sky. Quickly they noticed that while most stars remained fixed in their patterned relationships with each other, a few "stars" moved from night to night. Much later, the ancient people realized that there were five such "wandering stars," and that each one moved in distinct and characteristic ways. At some point someone realized that the moon and sun, although much brighter, were of the same family; they followed the same path as the wanderers.

Thus, the "seven planets" entered the astrological pantheon. Thousands of years elapsed before the invention of the telescope heralded the discovery of a new and fundamentally different family of planets—the invisible ones.

An astronomer might cringe at my calling Uranus, Neptune, and Pluto "invisible." They are, of course, quite visible—through a telescope. But there is a wise innocence about astrology. We concentrate first on what the eye sees: only later do we cautiously begin to apply analytic, cognitive processes. To the innocent eye, the outer planets clearly have a different nature and a different order of significance than the visible seven. We speak of Uranus beginning a new "octave" of planets—a musical metaphor we'll explore in some detail in the following chapter.

For our purposes, the critical realization is that throughout virtually all the years and societies in which some form of astrology has been practiced, the core of the system has been the play of seven planets against twelve signs. As we have seen, the twelvefold logic of the color wheel and that of the zodiac seem to be the same.

Is there a similar connection between color and the planets?

Hold a prism in the sunlight, what do you see? The same thing Isaac Newton saw when he did the experiment for the first time back in the seventeenth century: seven bands of pure color—red, orange, yellow, green, blue, indigo, and violet   the famous "Roy G. Biv" of high school physics texts. The colors always play out in that order, arrayed from the relatively long wavelength and low frequency of red toward the short wavelength, high frequency of violet. They are clearly arrayed in bands, and there are always seven of them.

Seven bands of color, seven planets. Again, the laws of both astrology and color appear to be expressions of the same unifying principle.

Some of astrology's vitality as a metaphor arises from the fact that it is not just a single system of symbols. It is actually two systems: planets and signs. Seven and twelve.

The numbers do not mix well. They make a strange multi-digit fraction; they refuse to divide comfortably into each other. They represent two basically incompatible ways of parceling out existential realities. Thus, "the seven and the twelve" force a complexity and an ambiguity into astrological thinking —a complexity and ambiguity that reflect the ironic, often tense, nature of human experience.

Color works the same way.

By starting with the three primaries, one can weave the spectrum into six hues, then twelve, and so on, as we saw. There is nothing arbitrary about it; the traditional color wheel reflects physical laws.

Then one can refract light through a prism, creating the band of seven colors—and observe another quite distinct physical law in action.

But how to reconcile the seven with the twelve? One can't, either astrologically or chromatically. In each system, the primordial truth—whether it is of human consciousness or of white light—expresses itself naturally in two ambiguous, incongruent ways. Novelist John Crowley in *Aegypt* writes, "There is more than one history of the world."

He seems to be onto something.

What does all this mean?

That the principles of astrology are more familiar, and more primordial, than most of us imagine.

That our minds are molded around them in as primary a way as the match between our eyes and visible light.

That our brains resonate with signs and planets just as readily as they do to the colors of the rainbow, and in much the same way.

As light breaks down into color, consciousness breaks down into signs and planets.

The two are one.

8

THE ARGUMENT OF SOUND

The *Bible* tells us that God created the world. That's one way of pointing our fingers at the mystery. But God is not alone in that world-building. You do it too. You take the raw material of the senses, interpret it, weave it together, make it make sense. In the end, you've built a universe and stored it in your head.

A lot has been written about the way each of us creates his or her own reality. Most of it comes down to this basic foundation: half of what we experience as the world is really an encounter with our own attitudes, expectations, and beliefs.

There is useful wisdom in that kind of thinking, but it avoids a question or two, such as how we humans can communicate at all. There is enormous diversity in our personalities. Were reality utterly and totally conditioned by attitude, we would be as alien to each other as an octopus and a goldfinch. Sometimes it feels that way, but much of the time it doesn't. We humans agree enough on the nature of reality to form communities and civilizations. There's common ground among us. Something links us. Something organizes our brains in parallel ways.

Eyes and ears. The senses. That's a big part of what ties us together. Rocks are hard, thunder is loud, to one and all, communally and universally. There is something deeper than philosophy in us. There is something elementally human, something we all share. I am not concerned with metaphysics here—just those parts of life we hold in common, easily, almost unconsciously. Touch. Taste. Smell. Sound. Light. The five senses.

And the spell they weave.

In the previous chapter, we saw how closely our visual experience of light and color parallels the logic of astrology. What about sound? Our ears define reality for us almost as basically as our eyes. Can we draw any similar parallels?

Do-Re-Mi-Fa-So-La -Ti- ...

If you've got any knowledge of music, there is probably a little knot in your stomach now. Go ahead, say it:

... Do.

Ah.

That final "Do" completes the scale. Or so it seems. In musicological terms, that is only one way of looking at it. The high "Do" actually starts the next octave. Thus, the ascent through any single octave of music involves hitting seven tones, not eight. Then the cycle begins again. The eighth tone of an octave is really the first tone of the next one.

Seven tones.

And seven visible planets. Are we again seeing the pattern we encountered in the realm of color a few pages ago?

Have a look at a piano keyboard. If you can find "middle "C," hit it, then strike the next six white keys in sequence. You've just performed the C major scale—and you'll feel better if you hit the next white key as well, completing one octave and simultaneously beginning the subsequent one.

But you haven't played *all* the notes available between "middle C" and "C above middle C." You've left out all the black keys. How many of them are there? Five. So seven notes were sounded, while five were left silent. There are twelve notes all together.

Music, as it's played in the Western world, reflects the same principles we see in color theory and astrology. In each one, there is a play of seven against twelve. In each, "the twelve" represents a kind of background field against which seven functions emerge actively.

White light (a mixture of all twelve colors) refracts through a prism into seven bands.

Out of twelve notes, seven are chosen to make a melody.

Against a wheel of twelve signs, seven visible planets move, triggering seven zodiacal points into active manifestation in personality and circumstance.

With color, we were on solid theoretical ground. The seven and the twelve emerge clearly there from the operation of unambiguous physical laws. With sound, as we look at it more carefully, there are some loose ends. Or more accurately, everything is loose except the ends. "Middle C" and "C above middle C" have a precise, physical relationship. When you hear the former, what is happening is that exactly 261.6 sound waves are hitting your eardrum each second. An octave higher, the "frequency" is 523.2.

The numbers are not particularly important—they were established quite arbitrarily in 1939. What is important is their ratio: at the octave, the frequency has precisely doubled. And, within tiny tolerances, the human ear can tell when that has happened. The tones do not clash; they sound harmonious.

Between the low and the high notes of an octave, there lies an infinite number of potential tones, just as the color wheel contains a potentially infinite range of shades. Why do we divide that range into twelve steps, then perceive a particularly harmonious association among seven of them?

I wish, along with most musical theorists, that there were a simple answer to that question, based on simple mathematical ratios. But that is not *quite* true. The whole area is extraordinarily complex, at least when we study it rigorously. In the octave, the ratio is two to one. Exactly. As we get into the intervening tones, we find only approximations. The ratio that defines the "Fifth" (The "G" in the C scale) is three to two ... ideally. The "Fourth" ("F" in the C scale) is four to three ... more or less.

The trouble is, if any two notes are tuned perfectly to their natural ratios, the numbers don't come out quite right for the other notes of the scale.

Throughout history, this musical problem has been dealt with in a variety of ways, always involving compromises. The whole vexed area is called *temperament* (think of Bach's "Well-Tempered Clavier"). Presently, we use a system called "equal temperament," in which the tonal errors are divided equally among all the notes of the scale. Nothing is perfect, nothing is too bad.

For most of us, these distinctions among "temperaments" are subtle, although trained musicians delight in arguing the merits of various tunings. This is one reason, by the way, that classical music played on traditional instruments sounds so different. Often the players are using a different temperament as well as different violins and cellos.

For our purposes, the key is that the seven tones of the scale emerge from simple mathematical ratios among frequencies ... approximately.

A five-note "pentatonic" scale is common in Chinese and ancient Scots and Irish music, along with some of the indigenous music of East Africa and Southern Asia. But, apart from those few exceptions, the seven-note scale appears to be an almost universal human invention. As Sir James Jeans writes in his book, *Science and Music*, "On taking the first seven notes, we have the ordinary diatonic scale, which seems to have been introduced in Greece in the middle of the sixth century BC, was standardized by Pythagoras, and has remained the normal scale for western music ever since." Significantly, he adds, "The beginnings of this scale cannot be traced. Garstang found two Egyptian flutes, the date of which cannot be later than about 2000 BC; these gave the seven note scale."

Most of us, even nonmusicians, are familiar with the idea that there are "major" and "minor" scales. Each reflects a different choice of exactly *which* seven notes to select out of the twelve. Some of us will have heard references to other scales, no longer in common use, scales with names that still sound musical: the "Lydian mode," the "Dorian," the "Phrygian," the "Mixolydian."

Let James Jeans explain it all to you, if you're interested in the technicalities. For us, it is enough to recognize that each of these scales has seven notes, and that a tendency to select seven notes from a field of twelve was almost universal even in very early times and in diverse cultures.

What does this tell us? That the human brain, quite instinctively, organizes sound according to the same "program" by which light, and consciousness itself is organized: the "music of the spheres."

Astrology.

The parallels between sound and the horoscope extend further. As we saw, "C above Middle C" starts a new octave. The notes in this second scale have the same names and the same ratios as those in the lower octave, but their frequencies are all precisely doubled. We might say that they are the same notes, but played at a higher energy level.

Something strikingly parallel occurs in the solar system. The "invisible" planets—Uranus, Neptune, and Pluto—appear to have an octave relationship with the first three planets beyond the sun—Mercury, Venus, and Mars. (As always, in astrology, we leave the Earth out of our considerations. We are sitting on it, which precludes its figuring in the celestial dance.)

Books are written about each planet, but briefly, Mercury is the planet of the mind—and Uranus is the planet of genius. Feel the "octave relationship?" Venus is the planet of human love and affection—while Neptune represents compassion, universal oneness, and God's love. Mars symbolizes our aggressive, assertive function, while Pluto represents, among other things, the altruistic impulse to live—or die—for something in which we believe.

Octaves.

In each, the metaphor that "the energy has doubled" rings true.

Sight, sound, and astrology: all three operate according to the same internal logic. All shape the way the mind comes to terms with reality. Each underlies every thought, every feeling, every action unfolding in the human world.

Like the notion that human consciousness is three-dimensional, we don't think about the Seven-and-the-Twelve much. Like height, width, and breadth, they are simply assumed and therefore almost invisible.

Sight, sound, and astrology—the program beneath the program. In every human perception since history began, they have left their mark. One we see, one we hear—and one subtly shapes the perceiver.

The physical world comes alive with "zodiacs" once we are sensitized to the wheels of colors, sounds, and signs that permeate our cerebrums. No two snowflakes, as every school kid knows, are exactly alike. And yet there is a very specific symmetry among them: they are all *hexagonal*. That is, each flake has six equidistant "arms," as though they were little color wheels taken only as far the primary and secondary hues.

That alone suggests a certain parallel between snowflakes and the logic of color, sound, and astrology. The parallel becomes even more striking when we take it one step further. Fundamental to the zodiac is the idea that signs are alternately "positive" and "negative," or "masculine" and "feminine." In looking at a snowflake, the arms can be taken as positive signs and the spaces between as negative ones, thus producing a true cycle of twelve—and countless trillions of particularly lovely birthchart blanks covering the earth each winter.

The cells of a honeycomb are hexagonal. Are the honeybees responding to the same organizing principle we see expressed in the zodiac?

Quartz crystals have six faces. So do emeralds. Diamonds naturally have twelve.

Even at the atomic level, the same pattern emerges. Electrons "orbit" the nucleus of an atom in "shells," each representing an energy level. The simplest of these shells, called the "s orbital," holds up to two electrons. The next one out, called the "p orbital," holds up to six. And there may be more than one p orbital in an atom. Looking at a diagram of an atom of silver, or iron, or europium, one is thus again faced with the snowflake-zodiac.

Carbon, the element upon which all organic process-es are founded has six electrons.

If only we humans had been born with six fingers on each hand instead of five, how much clearer all this might have been! And yet even the human body shows the snowflake form—two arms, two legs, one head, the genitals. Spread your legs and stretch out your arms: you are a zodiac too.

Why twelve signs? Why not ten or twenty? Astrology's critics often roll out that argument. They usually then go on to pronounce the zodiac a superstition arising largely from the chance factor that there are twelve lunar months in the year. (But there are really thirteen.) Or that the sun, moon, and planets happen to pass through twelve constellations as they journey around the sun. (But they really pass through fourteen, although the boundaries of the constellations are somewhat arbitrary, and were only formalized in 1930.)

Clearly, such explanations are insufficient. Our fore-mothers and forefathers, in their innocent wisdom, were simply recognizing in the sky the archetypal structure of their own minds: Plato's "Intelligence in the Heaven, to which our own intelligences are akin." Their senses washed by waves of color and sound, and their brains adapted to the physical laws which allow the mind to experience the world, it is no wonder that our ancestors tuned in so universally to the astrological principle. The wonder, to me, is that so many of us in the modern world find the idea of a mind-sky kinship farfetched and exotic.

And what is the precise nature of that mind-sky kinship? At last, we can define it.

The seven and the twelve.

Manifesting in light, omnipresent and eternal in the cosmos.

Manifesting in sound, resonating Earth's atmosphere.

And manifesting in astrology, shaping the mind which delights in the color and music of the Great Mother Goddess.

9

THE WHEEL OF SIGNS

The twelve astrological signs, as they are proffered by the idiot press, are a mishmash of pop-psychological insights, spiced with fatalistic prognostications about one's prospects in love and finance. We are represented as automatons, driven to act out a variety of embarrassing personality traits until our batteries go flat.

Such a perspective flies in the face of the reality of human experience. We change; life changes us. Are you the same person you were ten years ago? Who could be? Regardless of our attitudes and philosophies, one observation is sure: life, like the sea, crashes against our stone shores and gradually alters their outlines. Any system that describes the human personality as a fixed entity, cradle to grave, is transparently erroneous.

The signs, far from being immutable behavioral circuit-boards stuck inside our heads at birth, actually mark the contours of twelve journeys. In each, a goal is defined. In each, strategies are recommended and tools are offered.

And in each, warnings are given. Serious warnings. Life is full of pitfalls. Walk through any shopping mall with the word "zombie" in your head. See who lights up. That's what I mean by pitfalls. Few of us choose emptiness and misery; many of us find them anyway. To live well and consciously calls for more than good intentions and a positive attitude, although they help. To live well and consciously calls for something far more elusive: self-knowledge.

Novelists speak of plot and character as the two poles of fiction. That's a helpful way to think, but ultimately the two concepts are inseparable. "She's shy"

... but how does the writer show that? Maybe this way: "She walked hesitantly into the room, eyes downcast, and immediately sought out the one familiar face ..." Instant plot, in other words.

In behavior, character is revealed. In character, the plot of one's existence lies like a seed.

And if the plot is confused and ambiguous, what does that suggest? Confusion and ambiguity in the character—not always such a terrible thing, but dangerous if it's chronic.

Yet how can we avoid them? How can we, in other words, achieve true self-knowledge? So many false selves are grafted onto us, twisting the expression of our actual inner natures. Television does it. Parents do it. We swim in a stew of falsifications. How do we separate our own journey from the sea of irrelevant images in which we are drowning?

There are thousands of answers, all of them glorious, none of them easy. Years of meditation. Intense psychotherapy. A healthy marriage.

And, down the list—astrology.

Behind the endless variety of human biographies, there are a handful of pure archetypal patterns. Not all of them are directly relevant to each one of us. But several of them are. It is weirdly as though our lives, in their deepest essences, have been lived before and lived well and rightly. To gain access to that information can help us make wise choices. It can also warn us of those pitfalls to which we referred a few lines ago.

These archetypal principles are encoded splendidly for us in the world's library of myth and fable. The gods and goddesses of Greece, for example, are alive and well in Newark, New Jersey, once you turn the Toyotas into chariots.

Nowhere, in my opinion, are these fundamental human storylines presented more starkly and purposefully than in the twelve signs of the zodiac. There, the mythic principles emerge with the streamlined clarity of physical laws. Like the colors of the rainbow or the flawless tones of a Gregorian chant, they convey to us a message from another realm. They remind us of who we are and what we are doing, behind all those dishes we wash and birthdays we remember.

They give us, if we are willing to hear it, self-knowledge.

DETAILS, DETAILS

Maybe you meditate—or stare out windows sometimes. If so, you've experienced a transpersonal state, beyond the framework of individual ego-consciousness. Astrologically, one way of coming to terms with that transcendent modality of awareness is to describe it is an experience of all twelve signs simultaneously, just as white light is a fusion of all twelve colors on the wheel.

But as soon as you stir from your meditation cushion, as soon as the telephone jangles you from your perch by the window, you've entered the realm of plot and character. You can't answer the phone claiming to be the Voice of the Eternal. You can't chant *Om* ... You've got to act like a human personality.

Enter astrology. As soon as we are in motion, our actions are reflected in the positions of the planets at birth. Our words, our values, and the ways we express our characters, always, unfailingly, have direct correlates in the twelve signs.

All twelve signs are there in each one of us, but generally two or three of them dominate: the sun's sign, the moon's sign, and the sign that was rising when we were born. The five remaining visible planets and the three known invisible ones complete the rough outline. Each lies in a sign and each planet thus weaves that particular mythic pattern into the tapestry of our days.

The planets may cluster together in a "stellium." Or they may fan out around the wheel. Always, there will be at least a sign or two that is unoccupied, which is to say, less relevant to us.

Astrologically, in other words, you are more than "a sign." The boundaries among us are not so distinct. We are all as different—and as alike—as snowflakes, built from the same archetypal stuff, just differing in how that material is emphasized and expressed in us.

Astrology is a serious study, as complex in its own way as physics or meteorology. If you' would like to approach the subject in all its technicalities, I refer you to my own *Sky* trilogy, or to many of the other fine astrological books or courses of study available today.

In the following pages, my intention is simply to introduce you as briefly as possible to the wheel of signs, color by color, tone by tone.

If you are "a Gemini," what that means is that the sun was in that sign when you were born. And that definitely makes Gemini very important for you. But the moon could be in any of the other signs, and that's your heart. Unless you've watched *The Terminator* more times than is good for you, you wouldn't want to leave the moon out of the equations.

Learning the details of your own chart should present no problem provided you can discover the time of your birth. A local astrologer can help you out, or you can visit our website at www.forrestastrology.com.

However you proceed, I encourage you to absorb all twelve signs. If green were the world's only color, green's beauty would be diminished.

THE CYCLE OF TWELVE

In the following few pages, I'm going to attempt to convey a huge lump of knowledge to you quickly and efficiently. My ace in the hole is that you already have the knowledge! I just need to help you find it. The knowledge, of course, is an understanding of each sign of the zodiac, something with which you were born, just as certainly as you were born knowing how to breathe a mixture of oxygen and nitrogen. To bring up that built-in understanding, I'm going to employ a pair of techniques.

One is to zap you intellectually with an orderly, tabular summary of each sign.

The other is to speak to your heart and your human empathy by telling a brief story that, for me, captures the essential drama of each zodiacal phase.

To keep it all honest, after telling the story, I offer a second layer—a cautionary tale called "The Devil's Version." I am not convinced there is a gentleman "down there" with horns and a tail who lives to foul us up. But the metaphor is a useful one, as I think you will see.

A few words of definition before we dive into the material. As I wrote a few paragraphs ago, each sign represents a transcendent virtue. In the following sections, I call that virtue the "Developmental Aim."

Each sign embraces a path we can travel toward the full realization of that quality—that is the "Evolutionary Strategy."

Each sign supplies tools for the job. Those are the "Resources."

Those tools can be misapplied, producing a pointless, twisted expression of the ideal. That's the "Shadow."

Then there's the "Burden" of each sign. That is not another word for "Shadow," nor does it imply anything wrong. Instead, the "Burden" represents a certain perception, typically painful, which that sign alone must bear for the world. It's a dirty job, but somebody's got to do it.

By the way, in the tables below you will also see a color assigned to each sign. As I mentioned earlier, the link between signs and colors in the astrological literature is a mishmash of contradiction. I am confident I will hear complaints and corrections with many of my suggestions here. But as we saw in Chapter Seven, I am convinced that the color wheel and the zodiac are built around the same laws. True, we could potentially assign any color to Aries, the first sign—but then, unless we sadly wanted to abandon any connection to the color wheel, we would be stuck with the wheel's natural sequence.

Again, that is because these are physical principles— not just good ideas, but the law.

The association of Aries with the color red is pretty universal among astrologers and it feels right me. So I start there and everything else falls into place accordingly. Aquarius comes up violet, which is also a common as- trological assumption. Leo is yellow—but a slight tweak makes that "gold," which is also a familiar notion. So we do get some confirmations that we are onto something real.

But Taurus as an orange-y shade of red? Make of that what you will—but remember: if you somehow "just know" that Libra is pink and Capricorn is black, you have torn up the color wheel and decoupled astrology from its roots in color and sound. That's a high price to pay.

One more point. Artists have a wide vocabulary to describe various gradations of color. The language is lovely, but not necessarily very rigorous. Halfway between Red Aries and Orange Gemini lies Taurus, which is a mix of those two colors. Thus, calling it "Red-Orange" is accu- rate—but obviously kind of boring. I write "Red-Orange" here for the sake of precision and clarity, but in parenthe- ses I include the more "colorful" term for that hue—Ver- milion. I do the same for the rest of transitional signs.

ARIES

Color: Red

Tone: C (arbitrarily ... it's the relations among the tones that are meaningful)

Developmental Aim: Courage

Evolutionary Strategy: To go to one's limits. To seek stress in the form of adventure, acts of moral valor, or risk.

Resources: Adventuresomeness. Assertiveness. Capacity to function in a crisis. Pluck.

Shadow: Rage, selfishness, insensitivity, violence.

Burden: To see the power of fear as it shapes each person's life.

The Story

You've always secretly wanted to skydive, but you've also had an understandable terror at the prospect of leaping from an airplane. You run into a friend at a shopping mall and ask him what he's been up to lately. He says that this weekend he's going to do something crazy: a parachute jump. You light up. The friend observes that your interest is more than a polite one. He asks you to join him. You agree ...

That Sunday afternoon, you're hanging out the door of a Cessna 180, parachute strapped to your back. The pilot looks over her shoulder and says, "Any time now ..."

You're horrified. To chicken out would be mortifying, but that beats the pants off winding up as a wet spot on the ground. Then, your Arian energy rises. "To hell with it," you say. "Geronimo!" And you're plunging through thin air. The static line pulls: the chute deploys. A dream has come true.

You were brave. But you're a braver person when you land on the ground than when you climbed into the Cessna twenty minutes before. The experience has changed you, and the change will live on within you forever.

In the furnace of stress, courage has been forged.

The Devil's Version

You tell your friend, "Gee, I'd love to take that skydiving class with you, but I'm busy this weekend …" You chicken out, in other words. No one straps a parachute to your back. But all that fire backs up in you, turns poisonous. Two results: you turn prickly and argumentative towards the people with whom you share your life. And you get mugged six months later—with Aries, you're the Warrior, or you're the Victim. If you turn down the first, you get the second. No logic; just Cosmic Law.

TAURUS

Color: Red-Orange (Vermilion)

Tone: C#

Developmental Aim: Naturalness, Ease, Simplicity, Silence.

Evolutionary Strategy: To remain close to nature. To maintain stable relationships. To lose oneself in music. To touch and be touched. To establish one's position in the world.

Resources: Practicality. Common sense. Mistrust of abstraction. Earthy sensuality. Loyalty.

Shadow: Narrowness. Rigidity. Materialism. Inability to express oneself.

Burden: To see the unnecessary complications we all impose on ourselves.

The Story

Heated stones glow pale orange in the thick air. The scent of sage and perspiration wafts up your nostrils. Naked bodies in the sweat lodge, smooth and ghostlike in the shadowy dark. You recognize the faces; old friends. You breathe deeply. A sharp pebble digs into your thigh. You move it, and settle more solidly into the damp earth. A chant has started; odd, rhythmic syllables. You join in, merging with the sinuous flow of sound. The scene could be unfolding ten thousand years ago. Some things are eternal: flesh, stones and fire … and the human need for community.

Time passes strangely, obliquely. After a while you emerge, crawling from the lodge into the cool night air. All tension, all pretense, is drained away. You stand naked on the earth, a spiritual monkey, at ease among friends.

Someone laughs; you laugh too. You don't know why. You don't care. Life can be very simple.

The Devil's Version

You'd like to join your friends in that sweat lodge, but business is pressing. Maybe by working this weekend, you'll make that little extra margin of security and finally be able to really relax … maybe even get to Martinique for a few days later this year. And once there, you will find something else to worry you, some other reason to be living halfway into the ghostly future, tasting nothing and feeling very little here-and-now.

GEMINI

Color: Orange

Tone: D

Developmental Aim: A radically open mind.

Evolutionary Strategy: To seek the unexpected. To listen. To flood the senses with stimuli.

Resources: Alertness. Curiosity. Communicative skills. A quick, sharp energy.

Shadow: Chattering. Squandering time through disorganization and purposelessness. Failure to commit. Distraction.

Burden: To see the narrowness and rigidity in which we imprison our minds.

The Story

A soul stands poised on the brink of birth. The Lord of the Universe speaks: "I want you to go down into the Earth and recover your sense of wonder, your sense of astonishment, your sense of the miraculous." Inspired, the soul nods knowingly. Suspiciously, God adds, "Yes, I want you to go down there and try to get totally confused." The soul looks up, unsure. "Confusion gets a lot of bad press," says the Lord, "but it's actually a noble condition … a condition that arises whenever what we have allowed ourselves to see is three steps ahead of our theories. Go forth into the world and delight in your confusion. Flood your life with the unfamiliar, the unexpected. Cultivate uncertainty. I bless you with a facile and curious intelligence. Let it forever be at the beginnings of things."

The Devil's Version

Misusing the agility of the mind, the soul goes on to become an argumentative rationalizer, capable of proving anything with the facts … an unscrupulous lawyer … a dogmatic minister … a sleazy politician … a talking head … a volunteer guru on the New Age circuit. A soul is mistaken for a thought or an idea.

CANCER

Color: Yellow-Orange (Amber)
Tone: D#
Developmental Aim: An Open Heart
Evolutionary Strategy: To feel. To care. To nurture. To Imagine. To acknowledge pain and sorrow.

Resources: Sensitivity. Strong emotions. Healing instincts. Empathy.

Shadow: Voluntary Invisibility. Hesitancy to take risks. Obsession with safety. Disappearance into the role of caretaker, forgiver, and supporter.

Burden: To see the wounded child crying inside every man and woman.

The Story

You throw a dinner party as a way of introducing your closest friends to your new lover. Throughout the party, he constantly digs at you, criticizes you, makes light of you. Out the corners of your eyes, you notice your friends giving each other sidelong glances. "This is Mr. Right? I'd hate to see Mr. Wrong." The party breaks up early, a little awkwardly.

You're left with your new love, face to face. You know that his mother was an alcoholic who abused him. You know that he's never trusted women. You know that he has a knot of fear and hatred inside him because of that unprocessed wound from his childhood. You can, in other words, take a compassionate view of his nasty behavior tonight. But you don't! You tell him squarely, "You humiliated me in front of my friends. No one treats me that way."

You throw him out. Next morning, your phone rings. It's him. He wants to talk. You tell him, quite honestly, that you don't trust him enough right now to talk with him. You suggest lunch on Friday, take it or leave it. You tell him you've got some crying to do, and you don't want him to have the satisfaction of seeing it. Friday rolls around. He's had a miserable week to contemplate the results of his childish behavior. Half an hour into the lunch, you bring up his alcoholic mother. *He's ready to listen.*

The Devil's Version

As the guests leave, your new love says, "I liked your friends ... I'm a little awkward around strangers though."

You say, "Awkward? You were awful. I think it has to do with your mother." Says he: "You're probably right. Sorry. Will you forgive me?"

You say, "Of course I will. I love you."

A quick hug, then he adds. "Feel like going out for some Mississippi Mud Pie?" "Great idea," you say. (Exit the all-forgiving Mother and the eternal Child, arm in arm. Within weeks, sexual passion dies. Two years later, he marries a little ingénue.)

LEO

Color: Yellow

Tone: E

Developmental Aim: Joy, Comfort, Trust.

Evolutionary Strategy: To express oneself creatively. To perform. To earn appreciation and applause.

Resources: A sense of drama. Capacity to "read an audience." Stage presence.

Shadow: Noisiness. Pushiness. Insincerity. Childish egocentricity. The seductive dramatization of a false self.

Burden: To see the drabness we impose on ourselves, thinking it to be a natural part of life.

The Story

Six months ago you weren't sure how many strings a guitar had. Today you're practically Bob Dylan … at least, you've written your first song. But should you risk playing it for your friends? A half dozen of them will be here tonight. What if you screw up that F-chord? Or forget the words? Or worse: what if you play the song perfectly, only to see all those faces looking awkwardly at each other, wondering what to say that won't crush you?

Everyone arrives. Someone asks casually, "Did you ever keep up with the guitar?" The question disarms you; "I wrote a song today," you blurt out. Inwardly, you cringe at the words. But the die is cast: you are pressured good-naturedly to play it.

Nervously, you get out the guitar, strike the first chord, then launch into the tune, with Monarch butter-flies holding a convention in your digestive tract. You finish. People are glowing, blown away. One friend has tears in his eyes.

You've always loved these folks. But not like you love them now. And not just because they've flattered you; the reason is deeper. You showed them your soul. They liked it.

An excellent reason to love … to trust … to be comfortable.

The Devil's Version

"Did you ever keep up with the guitar?" There's the question—and your chance to take an emotional risk. You glance at your friends. You hesitate. "Not really," you respond. And the subject changes. But that pent-up need to have your spirit seen and appreciated doesn't evaporate. Instead, you find yourself talking too much all night, drawing attention to yourself, insisting on being the center of attention, but not doing anything really to merit it.

You feel childish and pushy, and you're right.

VIRGO

Color: Yellow-Green (Chartreuse)
Tone: F
Developmental Aim: Perfection
Evolutionary Strategy: To observe oneself with meticulous honesty. To log hours expressing helpful skills ("Salvation through good works;" "Karma yoga").
Resources: Clarity. Reason. A sense of the Ideal, tempered with practicality. Self-discipline. Helpfulness. An affinity for competence.

Shadow: Crippling self-criticism. Self-punishment. Fussy negativity. A sense of impossibility.

Burden: To see what is wrong with everything.

The Story

A woman writes inspiring novels for a living and she's proud of her work. She's also a compulsive gossip, and not very proud of that. Yesterday, while having lunch with a friend, she broke a confidence and revealed a naughty little secret about a third person. She recognizes what she's done and she's ashamed. That night she has a long talk with herself. The gist: "I love who I am when I write. I hate who am when I gossip. I write for six hours a day, which leaves eighteen hours for eating, sleeping and gossiping. From now on, I write for eight hours a day. Maybe gossiping will get squeezed."

Psychologically, this approach may not seem very sophisticated. She's not attempting to get at root causes and motives. But the approach will work. By controlling her time/energy budget, she exerts enormous influence over the shape of her behavior—and ultimately of her consciousness itself. She throws herself into her craft, and thereby lifts herself above her lower reflexes, a technique which the Christian theologians call "salvation through good works" and in the East is called *karma yoga*.

The Devil's Version

Our novelist goes home after the unfortunate luncheon, feeling guilty. But instead of having that long talk with herself, she suppresses the whole subject. The guilt remains, but now it's largely unconscious—a very perilous state in which to store guilt. Suppressed, it expresses itself in two ways: she becomes inordinately critical of everyone around her, making them the guilty ones, and she experiences an intractable "writer's block," which is her own way of punishing herself.

LIBRA

Color: Green

Tone: F#

Developmental Aim: Serenity, Peace.

Evolutionary Strategy: To flood the mind with beauty. To seek common ground with others. To cultivate the refined, elegant, and lofty dimensions of experience.

Resources: A tolerance for paradox and ambiguity. Aesthetic sensitivity. Empathy. Diplomacy.

Shadow: Codependency. Insincerity. Inability to accept conflict. Laziness. Obsession with pleasure and comfort.

Burden: To see the gracelessness to which we have grown accustomed.

The Story

The rhododendrons are in bloom, and the misty-gray sky bleeds mystery into their tangled branches. Despite the drizzle, despite the two-hour drive to the gardens, you've found magic. This is one of those "gateway days" in which our world touches another one: higher, loftier than the one we know. You walk down the path, reveling in the silence, expecting elves and miracles. You turn a corner: a waterfall, a glade of ferns, moss. You sigh. All tension drains from your muscles. The aesthetic harmony flooding your senses translates into serenity. You turn to your love, your friend. You smile. No words form. It doesn't matter.

The Devil's Version

You're miffed with your lover. Yesterday was the anniversary of your first date, and he ignored it. Why bring it up, though? It would only make an ugly scene. To cap the rotten weekend, look at that weather. We'd planned to drive to the rhododendron gardens, but the sky is ominous and leaden … why risk it? What if we get wet? Unless he really wants to go, that is. But you're getting a headache anyway.

SCORPIO

Color: Blue-Green (Teal)

Tone: G

Developmental Aim: Depth

Evolutionary Strategy: To probe. To suspect. To risk honesty. To make eye contact.

Resources: Emotional stamina. A taste for intensity. Psychoanalytic instincts.

Shadow: Self-absorption. Moodiness. Loss of perspective; humorlessness.

Burden: To see the seeds of decay and deception inherent in all things.

The Story

You've always had warm, spontaneous relations with your boss, but lately she's been critical of you. What's changed?

You're not sure, but you observe that she's put on a few pounds, while you've managed to shed a few. You approach her one morning. You say, "I'm not comfortable with what's going on between us. We need to talk." She's hesitant, invoking her busy schedule. You look directly into her eyes and say, "It's very important." Testily, she invites you into her office. You state your complaint and ask her what's going on. She gives a vague answer. You take a deep breath, knowing that you're risking your job, and say, "I've noticed you've gained some weight. What's behind it? Are you OK? I'm concerned about you." She flares, then crumbles. In tears, she tells you she's broken up with her lover, who left her for a younger woman "as skinny as a starving weasel." Your eyes meet, and understanding, connection, and forgiveness flood between you like an electrical current.

The Devil's Version

Your mood is bleak. You couldn't sleep last night ... again. Job worries: what a bore! Your boss, the bitch. She leaned on you again yesterday, as though you were an irresponsible twelve-year-old. Just like your mother. The other bitch. But what can you do? You sigh. You mumble. You go glumly to work and suck it up. Maybe you will suck it up for the rest of your life.

SAGITTARIUS

Color: Blue
Tone: G#
Developmental Aim: Faith
Evolutionary Strategy: To break up safe routines. To escape the tyranny of the familiar. To risk. To venture. To stretch one's horizons.

Resources: Pluckiness. Adaptability. Humor. A sense of the big picture. A desire to be amazed. Pattern recognition. Faith.

Shadow: Overconfidence. Irresponsibility. Insensitivity to other's feelings. Foolish errors.

Burden: To see the glorious possibilities to which everyone else is blind.

The Story

What does it all mean? Life, that is. You find it appalling how many of your friends think the question is a joke. Of one point you're certain: you're not getting any closer to the answer sitting there in your cushy law office. Sure, you're prosperous. Big deal. "Made money, then died." You can write your epitaph in advance. You go home early. You sit with your partner. You say, "Babe, we're rotting away. Come sail around the world with me." The mate says, "But you've never sailed anything bigger than a canoe ..." You say, "I'll learn. You'll learn too."

Five years and forty countries later, you sell the boat. At a loss. It doesn't matter. The trip was worth it. You re-enter the economy ... this time as a high school teacher.

The pay isn't great, but the work itself is—and besides, you know everything will work out.

The Devil's Version

Now you know why so many lawyers are cynical. But the money is good, and what else are you going to do? Work at McDonald's? Anyway, work isn't everything. And only damned fools worry about the Purpose of Life. You can fill up those empty spaces. Buy a German car. Hang out with the beautiful people. Maybe get married a few times.

CAPRICORN

Color: Blue-violet (Indigo)
Tone: A
Developmental Aim: Integrity
Evolutionary Strategy: To define basic values and live up to them. To accomplish Great Works. To let your intentions rather than your appetites shape your life.
Resources: Self-discipline. Common sense. Logic. Patience. Persistence. Self-sufficiency.
Shadow: Emotional constriction. Workaholism. Sorrow. Loneliness. Time-serving.
Burden: To see the illogic and inefficiency with which we blind and perplex ourselves.

The Story

You're eighty years old and getting around isn't as easy as it used to be. No problem today, though. Nuclear war wouldn't keep you in bed. You've got a retrospective show of your paintings opening at the National Gallery. You're going to make a speech and every word is going to quiver with the truths you've distilled from your life. Stick to your dream, you're going to say. As a young painter, there were times when starvation seemed starkly real. It didn't work out that way. In fact, you've become wealthy. But that's just a footnote. Now, at eighty, you know you'd follow the painter's path again, even if it meant waiting on tables in order to eat. Why? Not because it's "noble." Not because it's better somehow than being a lineman for the phone company. But because it's your path. And nothing is so precious, nothing else so close to the secret of happiness, than knowing your path, trusting it, asking nothing more of it than what it is, and following wherever it leads.

The Devil's Version

Retire? Why bother? Not that your work gives you any joy. Not that you need the money. But what else would you do? Watercolors? Painting was a dream once. Probably a stupid one. At least your career has kept your bills paid. At least you are not some kind of bum. Reality may be grim, but at least you've accepted it, adapted to it. At least you're not some flake.

AQUARIUS

Color: Violet
Tone: A#
Developmental Aim: Individuality

Evolutionary Strategy: To question authority. To overcome the need for approval. To seek out unusual people and experiences. To cultivate honesty and authenticity.

Resources: Independence. Detachment. Aversion to following orders. The outsider's perspective.

Shadow: Contrariness. Pointless eccentricity or rebellion. Emotional unavailability. Dissociation.

Burden: To see the pitiful hunger for approval that motivates most human endeavor.

The Story

God has quite a sense of humor. Imagine arranging that someone like yourself be born into a family of conservative Bostonian accountants! And what a near miss—you nearly became one yourself. You, in a dapper little suit! What a concept! Your brother seems happy enough in the family business, but that kind of life would have drained you dry. You ease the power down on the old Evinrude, circle the buoy marking the first one in your line of crab pots. You breathe the bracing air of the Maine morning. Two hours rounding up the crabs, and you'll have the rest of the day to work on your novel before Mom and Dad arrive tonight for dinner. The story is getting stranger with every page you write, too. A good sign: at least that proves it's really yours.

The Devil's Version

Why the hell does it matter so much to your hidebound father what your hair looks like? The clients—most of them anyway—only care about beating their taxes. It's just a boring accounting office, not a fashion show. "I'll fix him," you think. "Wait 'til dad sees me tomorrow. I'll frizz my hair until I look like a clown. That'll teach him to try to tell me how to live my life."

PISCES

Color: Red-violet (Magenta)

Tone: B

Developmental Aim: Self-transcendence. Decoupling consciousness from personality.

Evolutionary Strategy: To relax in solitude. To meditate. To imagine. To create. To open the heart to other people's realities.

Resources: Contemplativeness. Compassion. Capacity for fantasy and for the suspension of disbelief. Friendliness.

Shadow: Escapism. Forgetfulness. Self-deception. Martyr-like loss of self.

Burden: To see the hilarious pointlessness of all human enterprise.

The Story

That list of tasks will last until tomorrow, even without your attention. And old Cosmo, Lord of the Universe, doesn't provide too many spring afternoons as perfect as this one. Off you go, wandering into the forest. There's a little grotto by the pond, full of ferns and troll-shaped stones. You can sit there, unseen, feeling like an elf, for hours. So hard to say what you do there. Is it "meditation?" Sort of … but nothing quite so formal. Is it just "spacing out?" Looks that way … but it's more alert, more alive. Let the world name it, as they named you once. Funny thing about the world … how It loves a label, how it loves a boundary.

You watch the ripples play across the water, but no watery words ripple your mind.

The Devil's Version

Damn it! I just had those car keys in my hand five minutes ago. Where did I put them? I can't believe it's already three o'clock … I've barely gotten halfway through my list. And this is all I need: losing the damned car keys. Another perfect day. To hell with it. Tonight I'll eat like a pig, drink like a fish, and watch TV until my eyes pop out. I deserve a break.

10

IN PRACTICE

The laws of light and color, a little science, a few stories: have we "proven" astrology? Far from it. There are, in fact, many astrologers who believe that astrology cannot be proven at all. They may be right.

The scientific worldview, especially since the quantum physics revolution of the 1920s, is increasingly reliant on statistics. Patterns are observed: conclusions are drawn. The aberrations of individual particles are lost in the crowd, be those particles electrons or people. Truth emerges in precision only if we stand far enough back. As we approach the microstructure, everything turns cloudy. The improbable happens.

Trouble is, from the astrological point of view, we humans *are* the microstructure. We are the "quanta." We follow our own unpredictable pathways, stitch our own crazy-quilt. One person's response to Mercury-in-Gemini may bear little resemblance to another's. We are creative. We make it up as we go along.

Further complicating the picture, we recognize that no psychological function operates in a vacuum. Mercury-in-Gemini cannot be amputated from a birthchart and cultured somewhere in a petri dish. Inevitably, it is part of a living person, and its meaning is flavored by the position of that individual's Sun, Neptune and the rest.

In human terms, in other words, the smallest unit of full-blown astrological significance is the birthchart itself. A person. Attempting to investigate astrology with anything less is the same as trying to piece together the psychology of million-year-old hominids, based on their footprints. We can't do it.

The heart of the scientific method—and for most of us "proof" and "science" are kindred words—comes down to being able to say this: given these initial conditions, the following will happen. The stem breaks; the apple falls. The air cools; dew forms. Observe the connection enough times and you've got a physical law.

A crow lands on a fence; the stock market rises. You may observe those two events, but their linkage is not likely to repeat consistently, and so we deduce that they are not connected. The key, in other words, is repetition. Repeated initial conditions: a repeating, predictable result: instant science.

But in astrology, the "initial condition" is the birthchart. And birthcharts are unrepeatable. As far as proving astrology scientifically goes, that's the problem. It could be insurmountable, although in a little while we'll investigate at least one possible way around the dilemma.

In the span of human history, the planets have never aligned exactly the same way twice. A few minutes can make a serious difference in a birthchart. And even two people born at the same minute of the same day may well be born many miles apart—and that introduces yet another major factor. Why? Because at a given instant the sun may be high in the sky in one place and low in the west in another. The planets too. That changes their "house" positions, seriously altering the tone of the chart.

Statistically, one rule of thumb is that you need to observe patterns in at least twelve hundred cases before valid conclusions can be drawn. Ask twelve hundred randomly chosen Americans for whom they plan to vote in the next presidential election; you'll probably know within a few percentage points how the country as a whole will vote. The larger the sample, the greater the certainty. Theoretically.

To subject full-power, birthchart-based astrology to a valid statistical test, it seems we would have to persuade twelve hundred children to be born at the same place within a minute or two of each other. For this reason alone, those who say astrology "cannot pass the test of science" may be correct.

But they show a grave misunderstanding of both astrology and science if they then conclude that they've proven astrology has no relevance to individual human experience. The fact that it is hard to test or detect does not prove that something does not exist. Ask the physicists searching for the "gravity waves" Einstein's theories predicted.

The proof of the pudding is, of course, individual human experience. Does the astrological symbolism speak to you? Is it relevant to your life? Does it refer convincingly to the nature and timing of your experiences?

There is a long, impressive list of people throughout history who have thought so. The only real way to judge for yourself is to present a competent astrologer with the date, time, and place of your birth, and evaluate a full-blown astrological reading. Sun Sign stuff won't do; it's not a fair test. The testimonies of too many significant elements of the chart are left silent.

Still, let's not be too quick to divorce astrology from modern methods of measurement. I believe there is at least one hopeful avenue remaining for that type of inquiry. And let me be clear. I am talking about giving astrology a fair test from its position of strength—the full birthchart. As we saw with Michel Gauquelin's results, we can indeed sometimes see evidence for "single factor" astrological analysis. But I'm not talking about any subtle proofs derived from statistical analysis. I'm talking about proof that will knock you out.

Here's a way I think it could be done:

From a skeptic's viewpoint, perhaps the most persuasive dimension of astrology is its capacity to predict the timing of life's turning points. Planets move through the sky. Occasionally, they bump into sensitive parts of one's birthchart. Mars, for example, might one day pass through the zodiacal position that was occupied by Uranus at your birth. That's called a "transit." At any given moment, you're probably dealing with several of them.

Additionally, there are some predictive techniques which seem to measure a rhythm of unfoldment inherent in the birthchart itself. These are called "progressions" or "solar arcs."

Together, these methods provide the astrologer with an uncanny faculty. He or she can foresee the year, and sometimes even the day, when a person will reach various biographical milestones.

My personal guess is that the efficacy of everyday astrology will in fact be definitively demonstrated someday, and that transits, progressions, and arcs will provide the evidence. Here is the idea, with nuts and bolts.

My good friend Alphee Lavoie used to play hockey for the Toronto *Maple Leaves*. His knee got bashed, ending his sports career. Sad for him, but fortunate for modern astrology. He's developed several extraordinary pieces of astrological software. One of them, called *Star Trax*, is quite simple in concept. Sometimes a person's time of birth is known inexactly. The astrologer can then ask that person for a list of the dates of his or her life's turning points: marriages, job changes, sicknesses, significant births and deaths. *Star Trax* then runs a series of transits, progressions, and arcs. A graph appears on the computer screen showing where planets were concentrated on those critical days.

Some of the concentrations are easily explained: they coincide with known sensitive points in the person's birthchart, such as the Sun or various planets. (Those points don't move much in the course of a day, so we know about where they are even we don't know a person's actual birth time.)

But some concentrations are more mysterious … until we assume a certain minute of birth, which produces a specific time-sensitive "Ascendant" and "Midheaven," aligned with those concentrations.

Thus, the astrologer works *backwards through astrology's predictive techniques*, adjusting the birthchart until it would have anticipated those otherwise inexplicable events. The process is called "rectification" and I think that it will probably provide the eventual definitive proof of astrology's efficacy in scientific terms.

Take a sample of twelve hundred randomly chosen people. Ask them to list the dates of the twenty most pivotal events of their lives. The positions of the planets on these significant dates would be compared to their accurate, timed birthcharts.

I am convinced that the correlation of planetary passages with existential events would be evident to anyone who looked at the results. My confidence is based on the fact that this test, unlike so many others, would actually use the person's whole birthchart, rather than dissecting out the heart or the intestines in some misguided search for the soul.

Here is another test that could be done far more simply.

The "Composite chart" is a kind of averaging of two birthcharts. Halfway between my sun and yours is our composite sun, and so on. Composite charts are one of the staple tools of astrological relationship counseling. Note that in order to create one, we need accurate, complete individual birthcharts for each of the people in the couple.

I have a testable hypothesis based on my experience with couples. In happy stable relationships, there will be *a dramatic, and statistically anomalous, occurrence of Sun-Venus conjunctions in the composite chart.*

If that failed, I would be utterly surprised.

I am sure there are more tests we could devise. The underlying point is that I believe two errors have undermined astrology's relationship with "proof." The first is the grievous error of assuming stability in the human personality. The chart is a developmental path with many stages. That is what needs to be tested.

The second error has been "single factor" studies. The smallest unit of meaning in real astrology is the birthchart itself.

THE YEAR TWO THOUSAND

Some astrological events affect everyone, as we saw in our investigation of the sunspot cycle (Chapter Two). These events, typically transits, are the ones that shape history. Some of them are epochal; others merely give character to a year. Each person responds differently to them, depending in part upon the character of his or her birthchart. Yet together they seem to orchestrate the moods and decisions of everyone alive, and thereby modulate the flow of the entire human story.

In the remaining pages of this chapter, we'll explore an extraordinarily significant astrological transit which is soon to occur, and whose impact will be felt into the new millennium. We will look into what this event in the sky may represent for humanity as a whole, and make a limited attempt at relating those ideas to individuals. I say "a limited attempt" because, as we have seen, a complete birthchart is the entry fee to any investigation of astrology's full potential at the personal level. My aim is to provide a concrete demonstration of planetary symbolism based on transits, one that you can observe and evaluate.

As we proceed, I will make references to "people born under the sign of Capricorn." Certainly, if that's your Sun Sign, I'm talking to you. But in a very real sense, I'm also talking to everyone else. Why? Because everyone has some Capricorn in his or her chart … and the more of it you have, the more the Capricorn material I'm about to describe ought to fit what is unfolding in your life.

I am writing these words in April 1991. Watch and see, as we approach the decade's end, if any of these sky rhythms speak to the rhythms of your own experience. Then imagine their accuracy amplified a thousandfold by running them through the fine-mesh net of your full birthchart, rather than the wide net of a mere Sun Sign.

URANUS MEETS NEPTUNE

The planet Uranus takes eighty-four years to make a circuit of the sun. Neptune, the next planet out, requires nearly twice that long. So, like a slow horse chasing an even slower one around the racetrack, the times when they're crawling along neck and neck are rare: every one hundred seventy-one years, to be precise. It's an astronomical event, but it never fails to rock our earthly boat.

The last time the alignment occurred coincided with Napoleon's death in 1821. We're due again in 1993, although it's really more accurate to extend that at least a couple of years in either direction. As long as the two planets are within a few degrees of each other, we experience the characteristic impact of their conjunction.

What impact? As always in astrology, we start with abstractions and move toward specifics. Symbols lead the way.

Uranus, like all the planets, represents a particular circuit in the human psyche—in this case, our rebellious need to go our own way. Uranus represents individuation, which is the process of separating who we really are from all the dreams and nightmares our parents had about us, and from the trivial, generic life our community would graft onto us in the holy name of normalcy.

Neptune, in a word, is God ... or at least the image in which we make God. It resonates with that hunger inherent in all humans to merge with something vaster than themselves, something "metaphysical" or "transcendent." Classically viewed as a mystical planet, it is telling that Neptune often figures quite prominently in the charts of those who choose military careers ... and thus "dissolve" into a sea of uniformed faces. Dissolution, in other words, can take many forms. That which is beyond us, which defines the perimeters of our reality, is Neptunian.

When we're deeply frightened, we tend to turn unerringly toward our Neptune, our "God." For the alcoholic, it's the bottle. For the Catholic, it may be the Mass. For the scientist, the safety of logical reasoning. For the cynic, the bitter emptiness of existence.

What happens when the two planets meet? Humanity rebels (Uranus) against God (Neptune)—or at least against the current dominant and accepted metaphysical system of the society. That sounds a lot worse than it is. The God we kill at the Uranus-Neptune alignment is typically burned out and ready to die. It's not the Great Spirit we're talking about; it's more like the invented certainty with which we've been comforting and orienting ourselves.

The rebellion is stressful. People have the uneasy feeling that reality is falling apart. In a sense, they are correct, insofar as "reality" is always in part a cultural construction. Outwardly, there is chaos and breakdown. On a vastly more subtle level, *a new mythic seed* is germinating. The roots of the next couple of centuries are sprouted ... but usually no one knows that or comprehends it for a few decades. The collapse of the older *mythos* makes too loud a racket for most of us to hear the whispers of hope and regeneration.

Uranus and Neptune aligned in 452-453 AD, as the Vandals sacked Rome, putting a definitive cap on the *Pax Romana* which had given mythic structure and a sense of ultimate reality to a big piece of global civilization for a thousand years. "God" was killed ... and arguably the seeds of northern European civilization were established, although many centuries would elapse before they bloomed.

Two cycles earlier, a far more significant event occurred: The Roman Empire reached its maximum extent, coinciding closely with the Uranus-Neptune apparition of 110-11 AD. Another way of phrasing the same observation is more revealing: *Rome stopped expanding*. The enormous outward rush of its "God" reached equilibrium with the containing pressures of the "Barbarians." One can draw a direct line connecting that event and the sack of Rome, separated by a third of a millennium. In each case, "forces of chaos" dealt a decisive blow to an existing view of the world.

The intervening apparition in 281-282 AD saw Emperor Diocletian on the throne, and a vicious outbreak of sanctioned violence against the early Christians, as chronicled in every Sunday school class around the world. We are, of course, observing the death throes of the Roman pantheon in the face of the vibrant energies of the newly emergent *mythos* of Christianity.

Significantly, this apparition coincides closely with the beginning of Christian monastic life in the Egyptian desert. As is so often characteristic of this conjunction, the seeds of the new order germinate in the cultural backwaters, away from the seat of power and certainty, among "people who don't matter."

This brief consideration of the Uranus-Neptune conjunction in Roman history gives us the tools we need to understand the symbolic bones of the event. A "God" has grown powerful, perhaps too powerful. The "Barbarian," bringing chaos, appears on the scene to take that God down. A "City" must be sacked—and those who sack it originate in the "Wilderness," in some sense of the word.

Critically, as "reality falls apart," quite invisibly the "Seeds of a New Cycle" are established.

These are the archetypal ideas. Most of them have appeared vigorously in human history whenever Uranus and Neptune have come together. For example, the apparition of the years 623-624 coincides closely with the entry of Mohammed into Mecca, and with the simultaneous Christianization of England under Augustine. The following Uranus-Neptune conjunction in 794 heralds the Christianization of Saxon Germany.

In each case, the preexisting cultures were utterly transformed. "Barbarians from the Wilderness" appeared to "sack the city."

A dramatic expression of the alignment occurred in the middle of the seventeenth century, around the conjunction of 1650. Charles the First was beheaded. The commoner, Oliver Cromwell, effectively killed more than a ruler: he killed a notion which had dominated human thought for thousands of years: the "Divine Right of Kings." The tension and foreboding that must have filled the minds of the people of the era in the face of this event is hard to comprehend.

Meanwhile, quite significantly, in the literal wilderness across the Atlantic, the cultural seeds of a new, more democratic world order were quietly germinating. In 1647, The Rhode Island constitution separated church and state and guaranteed religious freedom. Maryland followed suit in 1649. Both Massachusetts and Connecticut set minimum public educational standards for towns above a certain size. Much that we take for granted today throughout a large part of the industrialized world was first put into practice then.

Arguably, the beheading of King Charles also set the stage over a century later for the "democratic" bloodbaths of the French revolution, and the comparably more peaceful American one.

I have explored this historical cycle in greater detail in my public lecture "Again the World Ends." You can download the archival recording of that lecture from my website. Here, I want to concentrate on its current climax. Uranus and Neptune align three times in 1993, in February, August, and October. What can we expect? First, we must realize that a more realistic view of the period in question would be 1989-1995, with the year of the precise conjunction representing a crescendo.

With that said, we look around us.

The notion that we are witnessing the emergence of a "New World Order" or a "New Age" is, of course, widespread.

Underlying that idea is the clear sense that world culture is in desperate need of some kind of new start. What works anymore? What is reliable? Not our economies, not our marriages, not our families, our societies, our political systems, our educational systems, our relationship with the environment. Not even our own gender roles. Nothing. Anywhere. As a result, there is a pervasive sense of fear and foreboding in the body politic.

I find it somewhat comforting to know that such widespread, convincing dread is almost always a feature of the spirit of Uranian-Neptunian times.

Theory and history suggest that somewhere, hidden in the "wilderness," new answers are emerging for humanity, born by "people who don't matter" or by "barbarians." What can those answers be, and who has them?

Let's start by going back nearly two centuries, to 1821. We can assume that the last time Uranus and Neptune aligned, seeds were planted. Not bad ones necessarily. But the mythic "God" who emerged from them has now become monstrous. We depend on him, and he is falling. Looking back at that God's birth, I see evidence that he possesses five heads.

The *first head* I will name "Techno-Science." In 1818, electromagnetism was discovered by the Danish physicist Hans Christian Oersted. Two years later, Andre Ampere founded and named the science of electrodynamics. In 1821, Michael Faraday demonstrated the fundamental principles of electromagnetic rotation.

Think back to last time your power went out; that's how dependent we have become upon this new God and the various little machines he runs. I find it extraordinary that in 1818, Mary Shelley published her prophetic *Frankenstein*, in which science creates a monster it cannot control and whose predations it cannot foresee.

The *second head* of the dying God I name "Heavy Industry," and the case for it is perhaps the weakest of the five.

In 1822, the first cotton mills began production in Massachusetts. I take this event seriously because it marked the beginning of so many unravelings on American soil, where mass production flourished enough to provide the world with a new archetype: the cathedral of industry.

The *third head* is political: I'll call it "Popular Democracy." In 1821, Napoleon died on Saint Helena. Could his death mark the end of the myth of the omnipotent, order-bringing world-conqueror? In the same year, Spain lost Mexico, Peru, Panama, Guatemala, and Santo Domingo. The following year, Brazil achieved its independence from Portugal. Dramatic events. A hemisphere was set free. Emotionally, I am inclined to view them positively. And yet everywhere today we see democracy's shadow: social chaos, a selfish preoccupation with individual rights and entitlements, violence in the streets, endless litigation, government tied in knots ... and an ominous undercurrent of hungering after "more authoritative leadership."

The *fourth head*, "Rapid Transit," seems simple: its full implications are visible only in the framework of the fifth and final one. Two events around the last Uranus-Neptune conjunction mark its emergence. In 1818, the first steamship, *Savannah*, crossed the Atlantic. And in 1825, the first railway was established. If you have ever sailed any distance, or walked, or ridden a horse, you know that such means of transportation give one a sense of having traveled every inch of the way. Each wave, each bend in the road, is an event. Comparatively, most modern forms of transportation present one with a very different sensation. We move through an abstract, almost fictional, space, only to emerge, somewhat disconnected, at the other end. Innocent, apparently, but put it in the context of what follows.

The fifth head is the fuzziest one to me; for that reason alone, I tend to think of it as the most significant. The new answers emerging at the Uranus-Neptune alignment are always radical and unexpected. Thus, the astrologer tends to look with particular delight upon the questions that seem to rattle and baffle us most deeply. Two events mark the seed: in 1821, Charles Wheatstone demonstrated sound reproduction. The following year, Joseph Nicéphore Niépce made the first permanent photograph. In contemplating these developments, my mind goes down a pair of trails. The first one I'll call the "End of Enchantment." Previously, the entire human memory was kept alive by artists: the tellers of tales, the painters, and so on. Always, there was a subjective element assumed in the material. Suddenly, we began to record our history "objectively," which is to say, one-dimensionally--that, at least, was the illusion. Myth and reality, magic and history, drew further apart, grew distinct, with myth and magic fading into the background of consciousness. Memory, both personal and collective, became mechanical; it no longer required imagination, nor was room allowed for it. Suddenly, there was just one mono-dimensional history behind us: the Cold Facts.

That's one observation; here's another: photography and sound reproduction are plausibly viewed as the precursors of film and television, which are of course ubiquitous in world culture today. And what effect have they had upon our collective sense of reality? How have they shaped our shared "metaphysics?" In a nutshell, they have "Made Reality Unreal." For a disturbingly large proportion of humanity, their most powerful and most frequent emotional experiences, and certainly their most interesting ones, occur while they are imagining themselves to be someone else. That's media culture.

Think about it: throughout history, the telling of tales and the attendant identification with cultural heroes was a ritual event, powerful and rather rare. When the bard arrived in the Celtic village, everyone entered sacred space. Now the average person spends something like a quarter of his or her waking life in front of a video screen. This *abuse of our myth-entering function* has led to a creeping sense of triviality and unreality in our personal lives, as though we must be "on television" to matter at all. Thus, a sense of shameful insignificance enters daily life. Our biographies become the stories of ghosts, with a resultant willingness to think of one's real-world actions as insignificant, one's body as unattractive, one's life and death as fictional, and one's relationships as disposable.

All of this is quite independent of any evaluation of the quality of modern entertainment media. When we consider the nature of the "mythic space" generated by a typical media offering, the case for the wreckage visited on us by the current culture-God becomes even more persuasive.

This fifth head—media culture—is the most perilous one, I believe. We have grown numb to the divine, mythic, or archetypal realm, leaving normal non-ecstatic existence stripped of much of its previous sense of purposefulness and hidden meaning. And simultaneously, a sense of hollow fictionality and abstraction has entered daily experience, as though one tap on the mute button will set us free. I am reminded of a cartoon I saw somewhere. An irate father is replacing a punctured tire on the family car. He's harried, the wife is subdued, the traffic is whipping by. The child complains. Dad's exasperated response: *"No, I can't just change the channel!"*

Who will slay our five-headed dragon? Men and women with one foot outside the myth. Barbarians. Chaos-bringers. People who "don't matter." Free-thinkers lurking in "the ruins of Rome," putting ideas together, finding alternatives to each of the five burned-out heads, making discoveries.

All these people have two qualities in common: a willingness to imagine themselves to be wrong, and an openness to the notion that any one of their cherished beliefs might be a lie. Those are the keys.

I have lectured on this conjunction at many astrological conferences. I always make a point of saying I am glad to be there and feel good about being able to share these ideas with people face to face. Then I point out that those very sentiments are strong evidence for my complicity in the current madness. In order to attend those conferences, I must conspire with a hundred other people to bum ten thousand gallons of aviation fuel in the upper atmosphere, wreaking God-knows-what kind of havoc on the environment. A farmer in South Dakota may well die of lung cancer because I attended the conference. And yet I feel good about being there!

Anyone who can help make the new myth is open to that kind of self-questioning. It is as though the individual life becomes a kind of microcosmic laboratory in which macro-answers are generated, piece by piece.

Who will generate them? Astrologically, one can give a surprisingly definitive answer. The alignment of the two planets is occurring just past the middle of the sign Capricorn. Anyone who is sensitive to that part of the zodiac bears the "mark of the beast," so to speak. In a sense, that means everyone. But if you have a planet located mid-Capricorn in your birthchart, the mark—and the battle—is strong in you. Capricorn Sun Sign people, especially those born between January 1 and January 15, are at the center of the cyclone. The conjunction is tied powerfully to the opposite degree of the zodiac too, which is mid-Cancer (birthdates: July 1 through 15, more or less). And to the perpendicular points in mid-Aries (April 1-15) and mid-Libra (October 1-15).

All these people, and many more, are experiencing "impossibilities" in their own lives, impossibilities which will peak in intensity in 1993. To find answers, they must recognize the errors inherent in certain of their fundamental assumptions. If they do, they'll have found pieces of the emergent answer. If they instead become defensive and insist on justifying the old, familiar perspective, they'll play the other side of the ancient drama … that of Diocletian throwing Christians to the lions. This is the ambiguity inherent in bearing the "mark."

So: again the Vandals sack Rome, again Mohammed enters Mecca. The sky is falling. Again. And something is moving in the shadows, something dangerous to all that has gone before, something fierce and barbaric at first, later showing the face of revelation. It moves, it whispers, not in fancy condos in Los Angeles or Paris, not among the "people who matter," but in other, darker, less auspicious places. The barrios of Rio de Janeiro. Soweto, maybe. Or among maverick poets, maverick scientists, wild-eyed crazy people with impossible ideas …

UPDATE, 2016

As I mentioned in my introduction to this new release of *The Night Speaks*, my intention is to offer the book essentially as I originally wrote it. One major departure from that principle is my update of the Sunspot material back in chapter two. The second one presses at me now. When I wrote the previous section about the epochal conjunction of Uranus and Neptune, it hadn't even happened yet. The book was published in 1993, right at the center of the event's time-line. Naturally the actual writing had occurred in the years before that, starting in 1988. In other words, all that I wrote—and all that you just read—was "prophecy" relative to the as-yet unrevealed meaning of the alignment.

Now nearly three decades down the road, we can evaluate the event from a sharper vantage point. Keep in mind that we are only barely into the full 171-year cycle. Keep perspective too: during the last conjunction, in 1821, humanity discovered how to generate electricity. How clearly were the implications of that development understood by, say, 1844? Nights were still dark and no telephones were ringing.

We are in the same position now.

But the handwriting on the wall is clearer now.

Subjectively, it doesn't feel like so long ago since *The Night Speaks* came out, yet I wrote the first sections of it on a very early, very clunky, Windows-based computer using a primitive word processor. Not long before, with my little DOS-based "Commodore 64" machine, I had developed an active business of printing out ugly little "dot matrix" birthchart forms for people and snail-mailing them the sheet of paper. We were busy enough with that enterprise that we had to hire someone to do the work for us.

I said "snail-mailing," but back then we didn't use that term at all. To me, there was only one way of mailing anything—that was via the post office. My little computer was not connected to the Internet. In fact, I didn't know what the Internet was. I vividly remember reading letters-to-the-editor in TIME magazine. Some were signed johnsmith@aol.com.

I wondered what "@aol.com" meant.

That's the way the world was back then at the onset of the Uranus-Neptune conjunction.

Launching into a long, obvious discourse about how the digital revolution has changed our lives would be tedious for thee and me. We've heard it all before. But that doesn't make the digital revolution any less epochal a shift.

Here's another potentially tedious point, which I promise I will not belabor: how do those of us with gray hair explain what that earlier world was like to younger people today?

That is what it feels like to live through a Uranus-Neptune conjunction. If you were born before, say, 1980, you know exactly what I mean. If you were born before, say, 1960, it's as if you remember dinosaurs. There has been a paradigm shift. A new *myth of the world* has arisen. It has happened fast enough to be shocking—and slowly enough that it kind of slips under the radar screen.

Not to flog the digital point, but think about GPS— the Global Positioning System that lets navigate strange cities as if we had lived there all our lives. We take it for granted. It was made operational in 1995, right on schedule with the Uranus/Neptune alignment. What about Facebook and "social media" in general? What about cell phones? What about Google and Wikipedia? If someone had told me in 1989 that I would soon carry a little wireless computer in my pocket with which I could access virtually all of humanity's accumulated encyclopedia of information while standing in line in the grocery store, I would not have believed them.

Then there are some purely human implications. Here's a giggle I saw on Facebook. *"Be kind to your parents. One day you will look up from your cell phone and they will be gone."*

Obviously the digital revolution has impacted family life and social relationships, and not always in a way that feels healthy *to an older person such as myself.* But who is to say? As we saw last time around with this conjunction, we created the roots of media and rapid geographical mobility. I'm sure there were older folks back then talking about how the world was going to hell in a handbasket too.

Let me go deeper. Not that my opinions matter, but I tend to be politically progressive—or "liberal," to use the old word. How you vote is your own business. (If we can't honor human diversity, we have no business in the world of astrology, amen.) But my Facebook feed is mostly progressive commentary. I don't get much of the conservative perspective, except as it is caricatured by other liberals or progressives.

Of course the same is usually true for politically-conservative Facebook users. They see "liberal jokes" a lot more than they see serious progressive argument.

On another note, I might add that I sure see a lot of astrological commentary on Facebook too. For obvious reasons, an interest in astrology reflects the people I have "friended" there. I also have a great affinity for Buddhist philosophy—and once more, my Facebook feed reflects that.

So, if I were to judge society by my social media experience, *the world is populated by environmentally-savvy, gay-friendly, anti-gun, Buddhist-sympathizing liberals, all of whom believe in astrology.*

In the same vein, I listen to my own music on my iPod or I stream specialty channels on Sirius XM. When I was growing up, Top Forty radio was very diverse. Now my ears tell me that everyone on the planet loves the rock 'n' roll of the period 1955-1985, hard jazz, and a bit of classical music—minus the operas.

See the pattern? *The digital revolution has fragmented culture.* The unifying impact of shared experience and a consensual interpretation of reality has been vastly reduced in the past three decades. Again, it happened so fast we are in shock—but slowly enough that it didn't register as change.

Going further with the same idea, I grew up thinking I was "an American." We still use that language, but how much sense of shared community does a right-wing radio host in Texas feel with an LGBT blogger from San Francisco? And, given the digital fragmentation of society, what basis do they have for possibly understanding each other?

Like looking at yourself in a maze of mirrors, the implications of all this just keep on ramifying. Connect the dots. Under the Uranus-Neptune paradigm shift I believe we are witnessing the *collapse of the idea of geographical nations and communities.* Where I once thought I was "an

American," I now basically think of myself as a "kind" of American." What kind? I painted it as a cartoon a few lines ago, but here is the underlying principle stated more seriously and broadly: *I now identify with a set of ideals and values rather than with a geographical location.* I brought up my "being American" a moment ago, but I actually have more of an active sense of shared values, shared interests, and shared experience with friends in Australia than I do with most of the people living in my little western town out in the desert. I even do half of my shopping on the Internet—no need to leave my house. And I am in daily contact with people in China, Turkey, and France with whom I have more in common than with my own neighbors.

In the post-Uranus/Neptune digital age, *identity is becoming nonlocal.*

Has this broadened my life? Or narrowed it? There's an essay question—one humanity is still answering.

I wonder how much the rise of extreme nationalism is a reaction against this sense of the old world eroding out from under the feet of people who are still attached to it?

Now, I am going to seem to change gears without actually changing them at all.

For Americans, the world changed utterly on September 11, 2001, with the attack on the World Trade Center. Before then and since then, other countries have experienced similar fates. Clearly, the rise of international terrorism has been one of the most obvious features of post-1993, post Uranus-Neptune conjunction, global society. What does the rise of terrorism mean? What is really going on? In response to 9/11, the Bush administration elected to invade Iraq. In the words of Richard Clarke, who was an intelligence and counterterrorism advisor to four administrations, "Invading Iraq after 9/11 was like invading Mexico after Pearl Harbor."

It's a funny line until you start the body count.

I am verging dangerously close to divisive political territory here, but I want to skirt that abyss in order to make a far broader point—and to distill the wisdom that underlies Clarke's quip. On September 11, 2001, *America was not attacked by a nation*. We were attacked by a group of people united by a common idea. That had never happened before. In the language I used when I wrote the earlier sections of this analysis, we were attacked by "barbarians" or by "people who do not matter." *But they were not a nation*. They had no homeland for us to attack in retaliation. In a classical example of "always preparing for the last war," my impression is that the Bush administration did not understand this absolute change in the *underlying form* of the human world. They felt they had to attack a nation because a nation was the only "enemy" they could imagine. So they "invaded Mexico." So far history does not seem to support the argument that this was a good idea.

In writing these words, I am aware of perhaps sounding "too American" to my international readers. Guilty as charged. Other countries have suffered far worse than America as a result of this spate of terrorism—this global war of ideologies fought by armies united, not by geography, but by common ideas. France is in shock and disarray. The Middle East has become a hell-world for an awful lot of innocent people. The "Islamic State" is presently looming very powerfully—and, in my opinion, it is doomed because they too are operating in the old nation-state, geographical model. Their recruiting, however, is utterly post- Neptune/Uranus. It couldn't happen without the tools of the digital age, both for spreading their ideas, but, perhaps even more pivotally, by presenting them in a socially-fragmented "bubble" with no reference to other points of view.

And that brings us right back to the Internet and the digital revolution. The civilized world is fighting a battle against an idea—and the neurons and synapses in the brain of that idea are digital.

All of this of course makes the digital revolution sound like a bad thing. That is not my point at all. Was fossil-fuel driven mass transportation a bad thing? Was the Industrial Revolution a bad thing? What about electricity? We may be rightly nostalgic for the good things we have lost, but I doubt that very many of us would turn our backs on the freedom, empowerment, and convenience those developments have brought to us. And remember: the roots of all those inventions lie in the previous conjunction of Uranus and Neptune early in the nineteenth century.

But under this new Uranus-Neptune cycle, we are now confronted by global climate disruption which is, in part, driven by those inventions.

In many ways, the previous Uranus-Neptune conjunction of the early nineteenth century marked the beginning of mass democracy. How well is that experiment unfolding?

What about the birth of media? (As we saw, the advent of photography and primitive sound recording, along with electrical communication over long distance in the form of the telegraph, marked the germination of media culture.) It would be easy to sermonize here about kids "helped" through puberty by Internet pornography. It would be easy to compare a live performance of Shakespeare to *Blast the Aliens, Part VII* playing at the local movie theater. Thinking about the current realities of "media culture," it would be easy to mount the pulpit and sound the bugle for "a return to the good old days."

But I don't want to do that—and not only because that is a bugle famed for its futility. Truth said, when we hear that bugle it is usually playing *Taps* for the dead and the dying.

The old world will not return.

Another illustration of that principle lies in the changing definitions of gender. Here's a line I quote from back in Chapter Four. "But certainly women, either by nature or by programming, have traditionally been identified with our intuitive right brain/left hand, leaving the 'more valuable stuff' to men."

I probably wrote those words in about 1990. When I read them again in preparing this updated edition of *The Night Speaks*, they seemed awkward and anachronistic to me. Much that was controversial and "politically correct" back then is simply assumed to be true today. Who today imagines women to be incapable of logic? And when was the last time you heard anyone use the term "women's intuition?"

I grew up in an age of activist feminism. The rights of women was a hot issue. Nowadays, many of the feminists of my generation are dismayed by the lack of support and appreciation they feel from younger females. The younger women, in return, seem to feel that the battle is over and they won, so why keep on fighting it? They are free to enter the workplace more or less as the equals of males. They are free to express themselves sexually as they please. They can live on their own and make their own decisions.

They are already, to use the common term, living in a "post-feminist" age.

I will happily leave it to history to sort all that out. Suffice it to say that the roles of women before and after the Uranus-Neptune conjunction of the early 1990s bear little resemblance to each other. At least that is true across much of the Western world. Again, this change has happened quickly enough to spin older heads, but slowly enough so that it is easy to miss the enormity of it. We older people see it more clearly than the younger ones since we have lived in both worlds.

But the younger ones "wear it" more naturally.

A similar, if even more dramatic, evolution has taken place relative to the acceptance of gayness as a natural condition. As with feminism, that battle is not necessarily over. But it would be folly to fail to see how far we have come. Remembering that the Uranus-Neptune conjunction was at a peak in 1993, consider the following synchronicity: On December 21, 1993, the United States Department of Defense prohibited the armed forces from barring people from service based on their sexual orientation. This policy was famously known as "Don't Ask, Don't Tell." I believe it is fair to take it as the point where the cultural tide turned, leading to the widespread appearance of sympathetic, multidimensional gay characters in the media, people being "out" without much shame or hesitancy—and of course, to the seismic shift in the collective attitude that has led to the acceptance of gay marriage.

Just to sharpen the point, let's go back to 1977 in San Francisco—a city famous for its openness to diversity. A gay man, Harvey Milk, had won a seat on the Board of Supervisors. He introduced an ordinance to protect gay people from being fired from their jobs because of their orientation and another one against "Proposition 6," which attempted to forbid gay people from being school teachers. That's the way the world was back then. Appallingly, bizarrely from today's perspective, people could be fired from their jobs for being gay. And on November 27, 1978, Harvey Milk was assassinated.

A couple of years ago, there was yet another bloody headline in the news. Just to strike a balancing note, I posted some encouraging words to my Facebook page. It was just a simple statement about how, despite this particular horror, humans are capable of progress and how we *do* get things right sometimes. I spoke of how far we had come in my lifetime in three areas: racism, sexism, and homophobia. To my shock, I got some condescending feedback about how racism, sexism and homophobia are "alive and well." *And, hey, I know that.* But I was born in 1949 and in the world I entered, racism, sexism and homophobia were actually, literally, the law of the land. If you weren't white, male, and straight, you were a target of derision, or far worse.

Anyone who says we are not making progress just isn't paying attention—or has tuned in recently, with an abject and total ignorance of society as it existed before Uranus caught up with Neptune and changed the world forever.

I once taught a four-day seminar about the world's current mythic changes in one of my Apprenticeship

Programs. One line to which I kept returning was simply "trust the children." I repeat it here. So many of the world's current problems had their origins back at the last conjunction of these two invisible giants, back when that unsung visionary, Mary Shelley, was writing *Frankenstein*. Children and young people today have inherited a dreadful world full of seemingly intractable challenges. But they are different from us. They hold the seeds of a new paradigm. Some years ago, they were often called "the indigo children." I don't hear that term much anymore, but the principle behind it was solid.

As I write these words, many of these human beings—born from, say, 1988 through 1995—have just touched the shores of adulthood. Most are not yet at full power. I have enormous faith in them.

I also have faith that they will shock and confuse me, and that's because I am a creature of the past and they are creatures of the future.

I have faith that they hold the seeds of answers I could never imagine. And of course, fair is fair—they are not all little saints, geniuses, and moral paragons. Many will just be members of a generation of lost souls, cut off from all that has given meaning to life for the past two centuries or longer. They carry an enormous burden. Some will break under the load. Even the best and wisest of them, in fashioning the new world, will surely, unwittingly, sow the seeds of many new problems—but let's not worry about that until 2165, the next time Uranus and Neptune align.

I suspect the scientists among them will begin flowering over the next decade or two—famously, scientists often do their best work before they are forty. Meanwhile, the painters, poets, novelists, and screenwriters among them, like fine Cabernet Sauvignon, may "need another thirty years to age in the bottle."

And these human beings will have children. They will have students and disciples, and the story will go on unfolding just as it has in all the previous apparitions of the Uranus-Neptune conjunction: old problems solved in previously-unimaginable ways, a world created that bears little resemblance to the one it displaces, new art, new music, new tools, new styles of relationship—and the faint breath of some unsuspected Frankenstein just below the threshold of detection.

What have I missed in writing this new section of *The Night Speaks*? Probably half of what is important—and half of what will be utterly obvious to future historians. Famously, what can the fish tell us about the sea? But there are two points I did not miss and which I feel are the practical center of everything: *do not lose faith in the human future*, and, above all, *trust the children.*

PART TWO

BUT HOW DOES ASTROLOGY WORK?

The solar system reflects the mind: the moon is mirrored in the still pond. How can that be true? Our hearts warm to the idea, but reason recoils. How can the human intellect make peace with astrology? Some say it cannot—that astrology is a Mystery, like love, which should be witnessed and trusted, but not analyzed. Pretty words, but they are words of denial. We are thinkers, curious monkeys. How can we make astrology plausible? Perhaps there will never be a final answer, but follow me down three roads of reason: Matter, Meaning, and Mind. Each travels a distinct direction, but each leads inevitably to an astrological universe.

11

MATTER

Earth, long ago: radiation raged, with no ozone layer to shield us from the youthful sun's reign of terror. The atmosphere, thick and windy, held no life-giving oxygen: only methane, nitrogen, and exotic compounds of hydrogen and carbon. There were watery oceans, but little else that might remind us of home. Except volcanoes. No fish stirred: no cushion of moss broke the harshness of barren, blasted rock. Embodied life, even extremely primitive life, was still a billion years in the future.

The date, put in numbers, is meaningless: 3,000,000,000 BC. Think of it this way: all the years in all the lives of forty million people. Or like this: if centuries were inches, the distance from Dublin to Paris. Or this way: if a human life were one hour long, 2500 BC.

A long, long time ago.

Something incomprehensible happened then, far from Earth. It may have to do with matter screaming as it was ripped from the universe and thrown into that no-place we call a black hole. It might be less exotic—just the exuberance of millions of huge, hot, newborn stars. Or more exotic: some process for which we have no name and perhaps no concept. Whatever the conflagration, we can still see its distant fires. We call it a *quasar*. Nothing in the universe has glared as brilliantly since time began.

In a darker, calmer place, one spring evening in North Carolina, a rather evolved monkey sat peering through a magnifying glass into a great concave mirror. He had a name for the contraption: "telescope." But he wasn't sure what to name the faint star he was contemplating. He checked his charts. Then, with that irrational satisfaction his species derives from labels, he knew: 3C-273. Not much as names go, but what a treasure to add to his observation logbook!

A quasar. The Mother of Light.

Such a muted thing. A dim star in the constellation Virgo, about a hundred times fainter than the faintest star your eye can make out on a clear night. But knowing what I was seeing made the blood rush in my veins: *I was looking at three-billion-year-old light.* I had never seen anything so archaic, nor had my eyes ever seen so far. Comparatively, soaring Alpine panoramas are for the hopelessly myopic.

Light, in one second, can girdle the Earth seven and a half times. And even at that incomprehensible speed, the light-stream my retina was intercepting was as old as that ancient, barren Earth with its methane winds. At a velocity beyond human understanding, the image of that quasar took time beyond human comprehension to arrive here.

That's the subjective truth; the numbers are a game at best, a vanity at worst.

Still, I always smile and think of 3C-273 when I hear someone pontificate against astrology with the old argument, "The planets are millions of miles away. How could they possibly have any effect on us?" That quasar, for all its remoteness, succeeded in creating biochemical changes in my cerebral cortex—a top-heavy way of saying, "I could see it." Certainly, my nervous system interacted with that unfathomable object in a measurable, objective way.

And compared to the vast distance of 3C-273, Pluto might as well be your undies.

The premise upon which astrology rests is that our interactions with the larger cosmos go beyond the effect of light striking our retinas. The statement itself proves nothing. But given the obvious validity of the principle as it regards our eyeballs, it bewilders me that so many otherwise sensible people dismiss astrology as "obvious" fiction, "transparently absurd."

Clearly, the evidence of our senses suggests quite the opposite.

THE PHYSICAL PARADIGM

Is there a physical basis to astrology? Will the actual mechanisms by which planets come to reflect our daily experience ever be discovered and demonstrated? Can it all ultimately be turned into equations on a high school science class blackboard?

No one knows.

The attitudinal trend today among astrologers, if I gauge it correctly, runs in other directions. Relatively few of my colleagues look to physics and biology for possible explanations of how astrology works. There are other, equally compelling explanatory models. Two of them form the basis of Chapters Twelve and Thirteen. My personal guess is that all three of the models I present in the remaining pages of this book have some relevance. Each is a window into the same mysterious house.

Of one point I am convinced: there is much in our turn-of-the-millennium view of the physical, biological universe that is quite consistent with the notion that consciousness and cosmos interact in extraordinarily complicated ways.

A fully scientific theory of astrology, if one could ever exist, would have to meet several requirements. It would have to "*work*," which is to say that it would have to predict rigorously a correlation between certain astronomical conditions at a birth and some subsequent dimensions of human experience. The principles of such an astrology would have to be *generalizable*; that is, applicable across lines of time and culture. Most elusively, to be perfectly satisfactory, the theory would have to describe a *mechanism* by which the astrological "forces" affect the human world. The last idea can be illustrated this way: we would need to prove, for example, that specific wavelengths of electromagnetic energy are associated with each planet, and that they have some provable, repeatable impact on the human brain.

Can we do it? Today, no. Tomorrow, who knows? As I mentioned a few lines back, my impression is that most astrologers working today show relatively little interest in this line of reasoning. And that's fine, in my opinion. Being "scientific" is only one of a variety of healthy ways of being human. But I suspect that one of the reasons astrologers generally shy away from science is that they're intimidated by it and don't feel competent there. By and large, we are more akin to the spiritual crowd, the humanistic and transpersonal psychologists, the mytho-poetic people, along with a welcome smattering of computer wizards to help us along with the math.

Another reason astrologers avoid science, I believe, is that we are so constantly attacked by scientists. That tends to create some "attitude."

Both those reasons are more social than practical. I personally see no insurmountable obstacles separating rational thought and methodical observation from the spirit of astrology.

In an amateur sort of way, I've been observing science for many years, always with an eye open for anything that might be relevant to an emerging theory of astrology. So far I haven't found that theory. And it would shock me if I did. I'm no scientist: in my reading, I probably miss a lot more than I see.

What I have found, and what I want to present in the next several pages, is just a mass of loose ends. Trivia, almost. Together, these ideas prove nothing. They are not a true theory. If they have any coherence or interrelationship, I see only a fraction of it. Yet, *en masse*, they seem to produce an intellectual environment in which the astrological idea finds its natural place. No longer does astrology seem so counter to the modern vision of the universe. Instead, the mind connects the dots, a bulb lights in the head, the lips form the words, "Of course …"

BRAIN/SKY

Astronomy, until the last few decades, was biased by an ancient assumption deeply rooted in the collective unconscious: the idea that the universe was a peaceful, eternal place. "Heaven," and therefore "the heavens," were viewed as stable, pure, and orderly, in sharp contrast to the messy world of men and women. Recently, that notion has been sent spinning. Our cosmos is emerging as singularly violent and unpredictable. Galaxies collide, stars explode. Everything began with a "big bang," and we're still toasting ever so slightly in the heat from that ancient conflagration.

All this mayhem floods the cosmos with streams of energy, and much of this energy arrives in the neighborhood of our planet in the form of "cosmic rays." Fortunately for us, our upper atmosphere absorbs most of the heat. Go about sixty miles up, and you've entered the collision zone. There, atoms and molecules are shattered—or "ionized," to use the correct term. This electrically-charged air forms a reflective layer in our atmosphere. We call it the *ionosphere*.

Now, picture Ella Fitzgerald shattering a crystal wine goblet on behalf of a major manufacturer of tape cassettes. She sings a high note, a very particular high note, which sets the glass vibrating. The longer she holds the note, the more energy is pumped into that goblet. If she stops, the glass is saved. If she varies the note, and sings even twice as loudly, the glass is saved too—and that part is a little more mysterious. The process is called "resonance." That glass has a "dominant resonant frequency," which basically means that there is a certain frequency at which it is disposed to vibrate. If Ella Fitzgerald matches it, the energy of her voice can shatter the glass.

Resonance is not limited to sound. It can be generated by any pulsing energy, which means just about all the juice in the cosmos. Here is our key concept: every physical structure in the universe, from atoms to galaxies, has a dominant resonant frequency. And if some other source is humming on that particular wavelength, however faintly, it will set the first object vibrating. Over time, the energy of the vibration in the second object will build in intensity, even if the humming doesn't increase in volume at all.

Confusing? Think of Ella and the wine glass. She hits the note. The glass doesn't break ... it only begins vibrating. She holds the note without increasing its intensity. The glass vibrates more and more violently, then collapses.

Like a great cathedral, the space between earth's surface and the ionosphere echoes with vibrating energy. The dominant resonant frequency of that sky-cavity happens to be about ten cycles per second.

Close your eyes. Relax. Be alert, but unfocused, not thinking, simply being. In other words, put your brain in neutral. Some call this state "meditation." Pulsing waves of energy are resonating in your brain. That's the famous "alpha rhythm," known for its association with rejuvenation, relaxation, and creativity.

Its frequency? About ten cycles per second, average.

A familiar figure. *The alpha rhythm of the brain and the resonant frequency of the earth-ionosphere cavity are the same.* They appear to be "entrained," to introduce the technical term. Thus, by the same logic that shatters the wine glass, the sky constantly feeds energy into the brain.

Why don't our brains shatter? Energy is bled out of the brain in the form of heat, metabolic processes, and thought.

The brain/sky resonance could of course be purely coincidental. And it has nothing to do with the planets, let alone the signs of the zodiac. Yet I find it intriguing, as though it is the first bread crumb leading us down a long trail into a dark but very astrological forest.

Let's say we might take it a step farther. Let's imagine that we found physical ways in which planetary energies interact resonantly with earth's own electromagnetic field. Then we would be on our way toward establishing the Solar System/Earth/Brain linkages that would have to underlie any physical theory of astrology.

There is an Englishman who has gone a long way toward doing just that. His name is Percy Seymour, and I am indebted to him for his trailblazing book, *Astrology: The Evidence of Science*.

TIDAL RESONANCE

Dr. Seymour points out that while all scientists agree that a variety of energies detectable on Earth are associated with the planets, they also say that those energies are generally so infinitesimal that they can have no significant biological or psychological effects. Thus, astrology is dismissed. Seymour goes on to prove that such thinking ignores the extraordinary power of resonance to amplify weak signals.

Take earth's tides as a starting point.

As every schoolchild knows, the daily rise and fall of the ocean is caused by the gravity of the moon and sun. Mathematically, those forces ought to produce a tidal rise and fall of about four or five feet, which is close to what we typically observe at the seacoast. But in certain places, the range is much higher. The Bay of Fundy in Canada, for example, experiences a tidal range of over fifty feet. Often, those extreme tides are explained as an effect of the shape of the bay and the sea bottom. True enough, but the real key is resonance.

It happens that the natural frequency of water's flowing motion in and out of the Bay of Fundy is "entrained" with the moon's orbit. Thus, by a chance accident of geography combined with the rhythm of the moon's orbit, when the water in the Bay of Fundy naturally flows west, the moon is there to pull it west. When it naturally flows east, the moon is there too. Through this mechanism, the moon's gravity, a million times weaker than the earth's in its impact on the water, has gradually amplified the tidal flow. Through resonance, a tiny cosmic force has been built into something quite considerable.

Percy Seymour has built upon this idea, and used it to construct a hypothesis upon which a rational model of astrological mechanism can be built.

Earth has a vast magnetic field, twenty or thirty times larger than the earth itself. The magnetic field has structure; Seymour describes it as having "bays, estuaries, and canals." And these structures have dominant resonant frequencies, just as do the Bay of Fundy and every other structure in the universe.

Many of the planets, but not all, have magnetic fields of their own. Venus lacks one; Mars' field is weak. But as charged particles of the "solar wind" flow through the atmospheres of even those planets, feeble currents are generated. By this reasoning, we see that all the major bodies of the solar system emit some electromagnetic radiation.

All such electromagnetic fields interact, however slightly. Magnets pull at each other, as every kid knows.

Thus, it is logically inescapable that Earth's huge magnetic field is influenced by the other bodies in our solar system. *And even when these interactions are extremely weak, tidal resonance can provide an amplifying mechanism.*

Does Earth's magnetic field vary and can those variations be traced to sources outside the earth? Emphatically, yes. Anyone who has ever witnessed an aurora has observed such changes directly. The ghostly veils are the earth's magnetic field itself illuminated by high-energy particles captured from the solar wind. The occurrence of auroras are linked to the sun's eleven-year sunspot cycle, which has an enormous effect upon our planetary magnetic field—not to mention its effect on human behavior, as we saw earlier in the book.

There are also changes in our magnetic field on one-year and six-month frequencies, changes driven by Earth's own orbit through the solar field. Further, variations have been observed that are connected to the sun's own axial spin, and to Earth's spin, and to the rising and setting of the moon.

There are additionally a swarm of other weaker rhythms in our planetary magnetic field which have yet to be investigated or explained. Are they related to the Earth's interaction with the weaker fields of the other planets? No one knows, but the idea is compelling.

What about the strengths of these fields? Even if they exist, can they be biologically significant? Magnetic field strengths are measured in units called *Teslas*. Seymour quotes a World Health Organization document: "The naturally occurring time-varying fields in the atmosphere have several origins, including diurnally varying fields of the order of 3/100,000,000 Tesla associated with solar and lunar influences on ionospheric currents."

Comparatively, most household electrical equipment possesses fields on the order of 5/100,000,000 Tesla, measured from a meter away.

A similar figure, in other words.

The critical question looms rather obviously here. Can humans respond to such tiny field strengths?

Solco Tromp, a Dutch geologist, writing in the *International Journal of Parapsychology,* 10 (1968), describes his investigation of dowsers—those remarkable individuals who can detect underground water through twitches in a stick of wood or a rod held in their hands. According to Tromp, responding to the earth's field is child's play for these people. They were observed to be able to detect fields of only one two-hundredth the intensity of your kitchen blender—or earth's magnetic field!

All this leaves out the all-important question of resonance. AC electrical equipment runs at about sixty cycles per second. If a given organism is not tuned to that frequency, there will be no resonant amplification. Ella Fitzgerald can sing the wrong note until she faints from exertion and that goblet will just sit there.

The key, in other words, is not field strength *per se,* but rather, the interaction between that energy and the perceiving organism.

The hypothesis upon which all this reasoning ultimately rests is that over millions of years, Earth's creatures have simply adapted to the electromagnetic environment of the planet, the same as we have adapted to earth's temperatures and the mix of gasses in our atmosphere. Our organs have become entrained to the pulsating rhythms of Earth's energy field, which in turn pulsates in harmony with the motion of the sun, moon, and planets.

We see some direct evidence for that notion when we consider the brain's alpha rhythm and its apparent resonance with the ionosphere.

Are there any more such clues?

A TREE GROWS IN CONNECTICUT

Harold Saxton Burr, in the 1930s, became interested in the role electricity plays in biological processes. Working at Yale University, he developed a simple voltmeter designed to monitor bioelectric fields. His work ranged broadly, but the part that is most relevant to our present concerns has to do with a particular maple tree.

Burr wired his meter to the tree and watched it for thirty years. The field potential of the maple varied quite a lot. Some of the variance could be traced to obvious electrical disturbances, such as thunderstorms. But there were other, more regular electrical rhythms present in that tree. One was entrained to the 24-hour rhythm of the day … and that could possibly be explained in non-astrological ways—for example, as the maple's response to changes in the ambient illumination.

Harder to explain is the observed 25-hour rhythm, which appears to be linked to the moon and paralleling the force that drives the ocean's tides.

Even more cryptically, another cycle of electric potential in that maple tree peaked every 29.5 days, as the full moon passed overhead.

The all-powerful sunspot cycle, with its eleven-year rhythm, was also evident.

Thus, a maple tree, which we fancy lo be dumber than ourselves, is clearly entrained to cosmological cycles. Its bioelectrical activity rises and falls in accord with astronomical events. Is there any sympathy here between humans and maples? The evidence suggests so, but before we get to people, let's explore a little lower on the food chain.

AN OYSTER OPENS IN ILLINOIS

Oysters in nature open their shells to feed around high tide and close them at the ebb. The mechanism seems self-evident enough: high water brings a rush of nutrients, low water the threat of drying out. The mollusks didn't have to be too brainy to evolve a way of responding to currents, water pressure, or any of a host of obvious signals about the state of the tide.

Or so it appeared.

Then Dr. Frank Brown, in an experiment that has become a classic, moved a batch of Atlantic coast oysters to his lab in Illinois. There they were placed in tanks and kept in the dark. At first they continued opening and closing in accord with their accustomed East Coast schedule. But then after a couple of weeks they became confused. When they reestablished their rhythm, it was adapted to *what the tides would have been doing had Illinois been covered by the sea.*

The earlier, "obvious" explanation that the oysters were simply responding to tidal cues was in error. It appears that they get their prompts directly from the force which lies behind the tides: the moon itself.

Next to moonlight, gravity is the most obvious force associated with the moon. Undoubtedly, gravity is what drives the ocean tides. It may well be that in reprogramming their feeding cycle, Dr. Brown's oysters were responding to gravity.

But it may not be that simple. The moon is also magnetic. Its position affects where the compass needle points. Quoting Percy Seymour again, "On average, over a lunar month the north-pointing field is deviated to the east as the moon rises, to the west when the Moon reaches its highest point in the sky, to the east again when it sets, and to the west when it reaches its highest point on the other side of the earth."

These variations are slight, but measurable. Do oysters respond to gravity or to magnetism? Or to both? Which astronomical force synchronizes them? No one knows.

What has become certain, however, is that many organisms are uniquely suited to receiving magnetic cues.

BACTERIA IN MASSACHUSETTS

Cape Cod's salt marshes are full of microbes. Naturalist Lyall Watson, in *Beyond Supernature,* reports a discovery about them which may have far-reaching astrological implications. A biologist at the University of Massachusetts, Richard Blakemore, noticed that these saltwater bacteria tended to arrange themselves in a north-facing fashion when he studied them under his microscope. Could they be responding to Earth's magnetic field? He contacted researchers in the southern hemisphere—and found that their microbes were aimed south.

Closer study revealed that each bacterium contained a crystal of magnetite that acted as a tiny compass. Throughout the seventies and eighties, a rash of similar discoveries were made regarding other creatures. Bees, tuna fish, salmon, green turtles, salamanders, pigeons … all have concentrations of magnetic material in or near their brains. In each case, researchers theorize that the little inner compasses do exactly what big compasses do: they help the creatures navigate.

Whether human beings possess these compasses has been an area of debate until recently. In May 1992, geo-biologist Joseph L. Kirschvink of the California Institute of Technology announced the discovery of microscopic magnets embedded in our brains. "They are little biological bar magnets" made of crystals of the iron mineral magnetite, he said. While hesitant to claim definitely that humans use the brain-magnets to navigate, Kirschvink added, "the presence of these particles opens that possibility."

British researcher R. Robin Baker thinks we humans can and do find our way around in part through the use of our own inner magnetic compasses. He devised a rather festive experiment to prove it. In 1979, he loaded thirty-one blindfolded students onto a bus and began a tortuous journey of several miles involving many turns. All the students were told that the helmets they were asked to wear contained magnets. In fact, that was true for only half the group. The other half wore brass bars, identical but magnetically inert. Twice during the journey the students were asked to point toward home. In Baker's words, "Analysis showed that whereas the group wearing brass bars could produce a statistically acceptable written estimate of 'home' direction from both sites, the group wearing magnets could not."

The results implied that our ability to judge direction when wearing a blindfold was disrupted by placing a magnet on the head. This in turn implied that people have a magnetic sense of direction. You might fairly call it a "sixth sense," although in this case it can be understood physically.

And of course some people "have a better sense of direction" than others. Might that ability be as objective in its cause as good hearing or a sharp sense of taste?

Baker's experiment demonstrates human sensitivity to the magnetic environment—a quality we seem to share with a great many of our fellow creatures. Unquestionably, a reliable navigational sense would have proven survival-positive for any mobile species, and undoubtedly, natural selection would have favored those individuals possessed of it.

But does magnetic sensitivity serve only one purpose and never spill over into other dimensions of experience? Are we magnetically sensitive merely so we can navigate? Or has nature learned to use that sense in a variety of ways, as it has with our eyes, ears and noses? So far, the evidence is sketchy. Still, navigational skills have little relevance to the survival of Harold Burr's maple tree, yet it clocked into the geomagnetic drum machine as well as any bacterium or blindfolded English student.

THE MAGNETIC MOON

Leonard Ravitz, a neurologist, writing in the *Annals of the New York Academy of Science* in 1960, reported that the difference in electrical potential between the human head and the human chest varies with phases of the moon, with the largest gap found at the full moon. Curiously, he discovered that while this pattern appeared to hold true for the general population, it was most dramatic among mental patients.

In 1962, Ravitz also showed that our physical electromagnetic fields tend toward a positive charge at the full moon—which rather elegantly explains the folkloric notion that everyone gets a little high at that time of the lunar month. Why? Opposite charges attract, so at the full moon our positively charged bodies attract negative ions, giving us the same "buzz" we often feel when a lightning storm ionizes the air.

Why should we be attuned to the moon's phases? From a physical viewpoint, it is difficult to explain. The moon remains the moon regardless of which of its sides is bathed in sunlight—and that of course is what causes the waxing and waning phases we see. Tides are phase-sensitive. As every sailor knows, they are most extreme, both high and low, at the new moon and full moon. The reason is simple enough: at those times the gravitational fields of the moon and sun are aligned in such a way as to reinforce each other and thus maximize tidal effects.

Something electromagnetic appears to be occurring at the same time. Ravitz measured it in humans. Burr found it in a tree. And, wherever biologists have looked, they have tended to find creatures possessing magnetic receptors waiting to respond to a whole range of electromagnetic signals, some of them phase-linked, others working independently of the moon's monthly dance of light.

WATER, WATER EVERYWHERE

Humans, as everyone knows, are soggy creatures. By weight, we are about two-thirds water. Lacking the precious liquid, life as we understand it could not have evolved, nor can we sustain ourselves for more than several days without a sip of the stuff. W.C. Fields preferred Scotch, dismissing water with a reference to the amatory activities of fish. But even his whiskey was mostly water.

The hydrogen atoms in water link to each other across molecules in regular ways, forming six-sided crystals reminiscent of little zodiacs. That quality is most evident in water's solid form: ice. But curiously, even a glass of water contains those characteristic crystals forming and dissolving, countless times every second.

Unlike most liquids, water can flow uphill through capillary action, due to the enormous strength and elasticity of these hydrogen bonds. And, unique among liquids, it expands when frozen. These qualities and others make water a wonderfully appropriate habitat for organic life. And when we climbed up from the puddles, we brought water with us, flowing in every cell of our bodies.

Unquestionably, any astronomical force capable of influencing chemical interactions involving water could have a wide range of biological effects. Giorgio Piccardi, Director of the Institute for Physical Chemistry in Florence, Italy, has demonstrated exactly such an effect. From his practical laboratory experience, he knew that the speed at which certain chemical reactions take place appears to vary. He wondered whether such variation might be due to something other than purely random factors. He selected a simple experiment: he timed how long bismuth oxychloride took to turn distilled water cloudy. He and his assistants repeated the experiment three times each day for a decade, generating over two hundred thousand observations. When the data were studied, it emerged that the chemical reaction took place more rapidly when solar eruptions had upset earth's magnetic field. He also detected a strong correlation with the all-important sunspot cycle.

Significantly, when copper shielding was placed around the beakers of liquid, the effects disappeared.

Again, we are far from traditional astrological territory here. Piccardi's experiments shed no light on the idea that a woman with Venus in Sagittarius is likely to become involved with more people in the course of her lifetime than a woman born with Venus in Cancer. But such experiments, along with all the others I have been describing, do suggest that there is a solid foundation for the notion that we are attuned to the astronomical universe in a wide range of ways, and that the facts of physics and biology are in no way hostile to the elemental premises of astrology.

THE MYSTERY OF BIRTH

In astrology, everything comes back to one critical piece of information: where in space and time were you born? The system rises and falls on the notion that something is absolutely critical about that single moment: birth itself.

Why? The difference between "a fetus" two hours before birth and "an infant" ten seconds after birth seems relatively minor. Certainly, the womb is permeable to many kinds of electromagnetic radiation—although not all and not so evenly, as we will see.

A question every astrologer has heard a thousand times is, "What about the moment of conception? Why don't you do a chart for that?" And it's an intelligent inquiry. Conception, not birth, has the best claim on being the biological beginning of life.

Yet birthcharts work. Something extraordinary must occur at the moment the baby emerges from the birth canal.

Subjectively, everyone with whom I have ever raised the subject agrees that "the energies" around a birth are wondrous; "something" fantastic and inexplicable is occurring. But what? And does it cast any kind of shadow through those narrow little windows we call physics and biology?

Dr. Bruce Lipton of the Stanford School of Medicine thinks so. In New Orleans in 1989, he presented a brilliant talk titled "The Biology of Astrology." The ground he covered was wide. For me, his most intriguing observations had to do with our immunological systems, which are as individual as fingerprints.

My own immune system is pretty tough, but let there be poison ivy within nine miles and I'm covered in the rash. I've known others who have never been bothered by poison ivy, but who have severe allergies to everything from dairy to animal hair. Those things don't bother me at all. As Bruce Lipton pointed out, our body's primary definition of "self" is immunological.

One way of looking at our identities is that we are all vast communities of cells. How do these cells, any of which could potentially survive outside the body for long periods, distinguish "friend" and "foe?" How does the self recognize itself? Why are we not allergic to ourselves?

At the biological level, identity is immunological.

Lipton observed that if he put a piece of his own tissue on a fetus in the womb, that tissue would be incorporated into the child's body. *But a few hours later, the newborn would reject the foreign tissue,* just as one might reject a transplanted liver or heart. Thus, a child enters the world with an extraordinary vulnerability: the immunological system is not activated. It takes a few hours to kick in.

Obviously, Mother Nature must have had an extremely compelling reason not to eliminate this terrible risk through natural selection. The explanation is actually very simple: were it otherwise, the embryonic child would attempt to reject the mother's body, with disastrous results.

Lipton says, "I believe that the bag of water, the amniotic fluid, the salt solution, that the fetus is developing in is an insulator. It prevents the electrical activity of the environment from reaching that infant until the moment it's born." He suggests that at the instant of birth, the child's immunological system reads the electromagnetic environment and "calibrates" itself. He adds that in his opinion, the actual biochemical processes which physically turn on the immune system take a few hours to unfold, but that they are set in motion when the child's head leaves the birth canal.

Again, in thinking of Dr. Lipton's insights, we find ourselves in a familiar position. Here is yet another observation which proves nothing but suggests much. Biologically, our separate identity is defined most rigorously and precisely by the nature of our immune system. And the individual nature of that immune system is determined not at conception but at birth.

That much is established.

But what defines the immune system, or "calibrates" it, to use Lipton's word? Is it really the newborn child's reading of the geomagnetic environment? We don't know. But we do know that one of the major distinctions between womb and world is that, in the former, we exist behind an electromagnetically distorting wall of salt water. We also know that the triggering of the immune system and the first exposure to the geomagnetic energy field coincide in time.

Just to be precise, it is important to note here that the salt water in the birth-sac is in fact an electrical conductor. Electricity is flowing electrons. Electromagnetism is a different beast. Light itself is an example of it. And electromagnetism is what Bruce Lipton is talking about here. I owe a debt to my friend and student Ray Ristorcelli for this clarification. Think "rocket scientist" and you are only a couple steps away from thinking of Ray.

Something quite pertinent to our identities does, indeed, occur at that mysterious moment we call birth. To me, the single most convincing piece of evidence in support of this way of thinking is simply that astrology works. We can observe that even if we can't really understand it. Conception is obviously an important moment, but the seemingly commonsensical objection to astrology's "myopic" focus on the moment we emerge from the birth canal collapses in the light of these recent developments in biological understanding.

Dr. Percy Seymour approaches the question of the birth moment from an entirely different direction. In his mind, nothing particularly critical to the person's identity occurs then. Instead, the child *already* possesses its complete genetic and astrological character. He or she lies in the womb awaiting the correct astrological triggers for birth. In Percy's words, "This trigger is 'tuned,' in the case of those who have inherited basic 'lunar' characteristics, to the lunar daily magnetic variation." In other words, genetic Venus types tend to be born when Venus crosses a sensitive point, and so on.

Thus, to Seymour, *our identities select the birth moment, while to Lipton, it is the other way around.*

Either way, the notion that the instant of physical birth bears a direct relationship with identity is inescapable.

SO?

So who knows if astrology will ever be "proven?" Maybe the question doesn't matter. I do feel that in the light of all the material in this chapter, the notion that "there is no scientific reason to take astrology seriously" falls apart completely. It is simply an attitude rooted in ignorance. Anyone conversant with state-of-the-art biology, astronomy, and physics must, it seems, entertain the idea that our lives and the larger cosmos are quite intimately entwined.

To the working astrologer helping his or her clients every day, these questions are curious, but hardly pivotal. The system functions; that is evident to all those who immerse their intelligences in it. Perhaps we astrologers are like the herbalists of long ago. We didn't know why foxglove helped the heart. We just knew that it did. Then came science, extracting digitalis from the plant. The human intellect, in a truly impressive exercise, began to understand more or less what was going on at the molecular level. Theories proliferated, each expanding on the previous one. Fortuitous discoveries occurred. New ideas arose. Science, that glorious flower of human intelligence, marched on.

But in the end it was still the foxglove, the heart, and the wonder of it all.

12

MEANING

"All right, I'll bite," I said. "Where is my wife?" Alphee Lavoie punched a few computer keys and began to meditate on the glowing astrological chart that soon appeared. Alphee, whom I mentioned in Chapter Ten, sells astrological software. We were sitting at his trade show booth at a conference in Seattle, Washington. He is also a master of one of the most ancient forms of divination—horary astrology. In principle, the technique is simple. One casts a chart for the moment a question is "born," then applies an elaborate series of analytic rules and procedures. Theoretically, the answer lies in the chart.

"She's not at home, but she's not where she's going yet," Alphee declared. "In transit, in other words."

I nodded. "Where's she going, Alphee?"

"The Significator is applying to the Moon … looks like she's going to see her mother." He reflected for another moment or two, then added, "But not just her mother. Some family member is there too … someone older, maybe a sister."

I believe in astrology, which should come as no surprise to anyone who's read this far. But even I was dumbfounded. I'd spoken with Jodie the night before. I knew her plans. After finishing with her last astrological client, she intended to drive to Raleigh and have dinner with her mother. Her older sister was in town too, visiting from Atlanta. I looked at my watch. If her day had gone according to plan, she'd be on the road at that very moment.

Later that night I phoned her. She confirmed the accuracy of Alphee's statements.

Horary astrology has been around in one form or another since prehistory. It might be the oldest branch of the art. The first shaman who said, "Jupiter is nearing Aldebaran; there will be many buffalo," was practicing horary. The discipline reached a heyday during the medieval period, then slipped into relative obscurity until fairly recently. Its rules are rigorous and its procedures technical. Much in the system is quite distinct from the methods we use to analyze a birthchart. The tone of horary astrology, and the scope of its inquiries, tend to be practical. Where did I leave the car keys? Will I get the job? Will my brother's cat be found alive?

I personally have limited experience with the technique, although I know enough to be impressed with its utility. Those who practice it seriously tell some astonishing tales. A businessman asked Alphee Lavoie, "Should I go to Las Vegas next week to gamble?" A couple of weeks later, Alphee got a check in the mail. It was "his share of the winnings." He used it to buy a new pickup truck.

In the previous chapter, we explored the possibility that there may be a physical basis to astrology. We made the case that there is considerable scientific evidence that our brains and bodies interact directly with the solar system.

But nothing we've seen so far can explain how Alphee knew my wife was on her way to visit her mother.

Why? That's because horary astrology *assumes no receiving organism.* What is "born" is not an infant, rife with brain waves, cellular chemistry, and an emerging immune system. What is born is only a question—even one asked idly, out of curiosity. "Where is my wife?" I'd taught a class at the conference that afternoon and attended a couple of others. Dinner was half an hour away. I had wandered down from my room at the hotel, strolled aimlessly into the trade show, sat down with my friend and began to shoot the breeze. A couple of customers had come by. I'd shut my mouth and let Alphee make his pitch to them. Then, very casually, a question entered my mind. "I wonder if he could tell me where Jodie is?"

The computer immediately froze the planets as they were surrounding Seattle at that moment.

And in them lay the answer to my question.

It is completely mind-boggling.

We can go further. Corporations have birthcharts. So do cities and nations. And relationships. Essentially, anything which comes into existence at a discrete moment of time can be understood astrologically. With or without a body.

People immersed in the techno-scientific mythology of our times are generally opposed to astrology. Their opposition tends to be emotional, even phobic, as we explored in the early chapters of this book. We can however imagine that if there emerged a true theory of astrology based on magnetic resonance between the human brain and the tides in earth's magnetosphere, and that if such a theory were proven to be scientifically valid, astrology could be absorbed wholly into the modern worldview. Physical forces would be demonstrated to have physical effects. Nothing in the foundation of science would be rattled. Predictably, many older scientists would mutter and object, while most of the younger ones shrugged and added a new wonder to their storehouse of wonders. It happened that way with the theory of relativity and with quantum mechanics. Likely, it would happen that way again with such a theory of astrological influence.

But horary astrology is an entirely different beast. There, the planets cannot "act upon" anything.

Nothing is there for them to touch.

DIVINATION

The Lakota medicine man studies the clouds: "My son is dead," he says. The Taoist sage in ancient China tosses the yarrow sticks, sets up the I CHING hexagrams. "Your daughter will recover." The tarot deck is cut three times, shuffled, then cut three times again. The cards are laid out. The gypsy studies them. "A black-haired man of slight build stole the money. You will not recover it."

Nothing I learned in Sunday school or high school chemistry class taught me to take such divinations seriously. Yet they often prove accurate. Anyone who is curious enough about those traditions to grant them even a casual investigation is likely to have an amazing story or two to tell.

The shape of clouds, the fall of yarrow sticks, the pattern of tarot cards—all are so-called "random" events. There is no conceivable way the "black-haired man" could have affected the order of those shuffled cards. My horary question in Seattle raises similar conundrums. How could there be any interaction between the planets as they appeared at a certain moment over Seattle and the social schedule of a woman a continent away? Yet, through divination, answers appear.

Divination. Perhaps the word itself is the key. The *Oxford English Dictionary* defines the verb "to divine" as: "To make out or interpret by supernatural or magical insight (what is hidden, obscure, or unintelligible to ordinary faculties)."

True enough, but this definition is missing a very obvious point. "Divinity" is an attribute of Spirit. "To divine" is to ascertain the will of Spirit in a given moment. Or to employ Spirit's own perceptual faculties.

Not a very scientific notion.

But the efficacy of horary astrology and its cousins suggests that perhaps the universe is not so quick to bow before the laws of cause and effect as we have been taught to believe. Other principles seem to be at work, principles which lie outside our current version of common sense. These principles were apparently evident to our ancestors, who generated an intellectual climate in which the idea of divination violated no taboos.

Then, for a while, the principles were lost, at least among educated people. It took a genius to rediscover them.

SYNCHRONICITY

Carl Jung, early in his career, "kept on coming across connections which I simply could not explain as chance groupings or 'runs.' What I found were 'coincidences' which were connected so meaningfully that their 'chance' concurrence would represent a degree of improbability that would have to be expressed by an astronomical figure." Working with physicist Wolfgang Pauli, he refined the concept, which they called "synchronicity." Jung came to view it as one of the fundamental laws of the universe.

Carl Jung was essentially a scientist and always viewed himself at least partly in those terms. "Synchronicity," he wrote, "is not a philosophical view but an empirical concept which postulates an intellectually necessary principle."

He could not, in other words, adequately explain what he observed in life without it.

When you think about it, you probably can't explain your own observations without synchronicity either. How often have you encountered "amazing coincidences?" Often enough probably that you are no longer deeply amazed by them.

My former wife had a roommate in college with whom she lost contact. I had never met her. Years later, I received a letter from the woman requesting an astrological reading. The note said she'd heard about my work "through friends." She had no idea I was then married to her long-lost roommate. My wife recognized the name on my notepad and immediately phoned her. A rather astounding tale emerged.

Years earlier, while traveling in India, the friend had struck up an acquaintance with a couple from Pennsylvania. Later, back in America, they'd exchanged visits. This couple, whom neither my wife nor I knew, was then sharing a home with a third person—an old friend of mine from high school, who became attracted to the errant roommate. He had, in fact, visited us a month or so before the fateful letter arrived, and while here, he had spoken glowingly of "this chick from Maryland" (this was a long time ago).

My wife and I had even listened as he spoke to her on the phone in our living room, no one having the slightest intimation that he was speaking to a woman with whom one of us had lived for a year.

He, of course, was the "friend" who had told her of my astrological work.

What are the odds against such a story happening? Dozens of long shots had to materialize to allow the reconnecting of two friends, the crown jewel among them a chance encounter between strangers traveling in India. Yet it happened. "Coincidence" is the word we trot out. Or "chance." Or luck. Carl Jung would let the words stand. He'd just tell us to look at them a little harder.

"Coincidence," as the word is customarily used, suggests the statistically normal occurrence of a rare event. Saying the odds against something are a million to one actually means that the event is certain to occur … just don't hold your breath. Which is how conventional wisdom would deal with the tale I've just recounted: it was a coincidence, improbable, but not inexplicable.

What *is* utterly inexplicable, at least from the viewpoint of conventional wisdom, is that such improbable events are, in fact, all too common. Virtually everyone has such a story to tell. Jung, being a practicing psychologist, heard enough such accounts to compel him to postulate the existence of synchronicity—a principle he laid next to our more familiar concept of causality, which is simply the idea that events happen because something "makes" them happen.

Basically, Jung suggested that events occur in our universe for either of two reasons:

(1) *Something causes them to happen.*

Or

(2) *It would be meaningful for them to occur.*

"Meaning," that perfectly human notion, thus takes its place in the Jungian universe next to gravity, the laws of thermodynamics, and electromagnetism. There is it seems absolutely no common sense in this idea at all. Jung himself was nervous about it. "I am only too conscious that synchronicity is a highly abstract and 'irrepresentable' quantity," he wrote.

Evidence is, of course, the key. If synchronicity is more than a pretty word, we need some proof that it is real. Countless coincidences. A dozen stories in the lives of each of billions of people, past and present.

If we could hear them all at once, that would be our proof. Or so thought Carl Jung.

Horary astrology provides another piece of evidence. It often works. Unlike the personal birthchart, we cannot begin to explain its effectiveness in causal terms. Even if planetary forces "caused" me to wonder about my wife's location at that particular moment in Seattle, no conceivable line of causal reasoning can account for how the planets "knew" where she actually was.

Yet, it was "meaningful" for me to ask the question then, and the answer I received was also meaningful.

Similar arguments can be brought forth regarding the meaningful arrangement of clouds for that Lakota medicine man. Or the Taoist's yarrow sticks or the gypsy's cards. All divination emerges as nothing less than ancient technology designed to tap the synchronistic potential of each moment of time.

There is another line of evidence for synchronicity, one that is actually taking shape on science's own cutting edge. It is no accident that Jung, in developing his theories of synchronicity, felt compelled to work with Pauli, a physicist.

THE QUANTUM UNIVERSE

Here's a little piece of science designed to make astrologers, poets, and mystics smile. If you don't have a head for physics, hang in there with me for a few paragraphs. I guarantee it will be worth it.

Cut a razor slit in a piece of cardboard. Shine a light through it onto a white wall. What do you see?

A blurry, circular patch of light.

Cut a big, square hole in the cardboard, and repeat the experiment. What you get is a big, square, sharp-edged patch of light. The blurry edges in the first experiment are called a *defraction pattern.* They only arise when any wave-pattern flows through a hole that's smaller than the waves themselves.

Think of ocean waves crashing through a narrow inlet into a wide, shallow bay. They fan out as they enter the quiet water. Light waves do the same; they fan out, producing that blurry edge. But only when we shine the light through the razor slit. It doesn't work with windows or other big openings.

Now take the cardboard from the first experiment, the one with a single razor slit. Cut a second slit in it, parallel to the first. Again, turn on the light. What appears on the wall now is more interesting: alternating bands of light and darkness, with the central bands brightest. This less expected result is called an *interference pattern*. What causes it is that the waves emerging from each slit sometimes reinforce, other times cancel each other.

Toss two stones into still water; watch the wave patterns interact. You'll see the same phenomenon. With light waves, where waves from one slit coincide with waves from the other, we see extra-bright light. Where a trough from one side coincides with a wave from the other side, they cancel and we see darkness.

If any of this is unclear, I encourage you to read it again. Why? Because here is where we leave our fictional world of "common sense" and enter the fantastical world of what is actually real.

Repeat the first experiment, this time using a device that emits just a lone photon of light. Shoot it through the single razor-slit. By chance, the photon happens to hit the wall in a place that would have been a dark band had we been using two slits. This is no surprise; remember that in our first experiment, we produced a big, diffuse circle of light. Presumably, light passing through the single slit is "randomized" and forms the blurry patch. A single photon could reasonably be expected to land anywhere on that part of the wall.

Now repeat that last step. Shoot one photon through the same slit. But first make one tiny, seemingly irrelevant adjustment: reopen the second slit. What happens?

The photon lands in an area that would have coincided with a bright band.

Do the experiment a million times. As long as the second slit is open, the photon will never, ever, land in a "dark" area.

In other words, the light passing through one slit seems to "know" whether the other slit is opened or closed! As Gary Zukav writes in his epochal *The Dancing Wu Li Masters*, "The question is, assuming that a single photon goes through one of the two slits, how does it know whether or not the other slit is open? Somehow it does. An interference pattern always forms when we open both slits, and it never forms when we close one of the slits."

Those pedestrian, wonderless "hard-headed rationalists" who always seem on the verge of forming the words, "Now, be reasonable, dear," hate this stuff. And this "stuff" is called *quantum mechanics*. Our photon experiment is just one example of the kind of observation that led physicists to realize that our "reasonable" ways of understanding the universe were hopelessly flawed. Since the 1920s, quantum theory has been standing any narrow definition of "rationality" on its ears. And no theory in the history of physics has ever worked so well. As Gary Zukav says, "Quantum mechanics is *the* theory. It has explained everything from subatomic particles to transistors to stellar energy. It has never failed. It has no competition."

And what is the essential premise of quantum theory? That no natural law is ever one hundred percent binding;

that the universe operates by probabilities, not certainties. In the words of Carl Jung, "The philosophical principle that underlies our conception of natural laws is causality. But if the connection between cause and effect turns out to be only statistically valid and only relatively true, then the causal principle is only of relative use for explaining natural processes and therefore presupposes the existence of one or more other factors which would be necessary for an explanation."

He adds, "This is as much as to say that the connection of events may in certain circumstances be other than causal, and requires another principle of explanation."

To Jung, that principle is synchronicity.

The opening of the second slit coincides meaningfully with a particular behavior on the part of the photon. Its behavior is thus a "coincidence." There is an almost overwhelming temptation to say that opening the second slit "causes" the photon to follow an altered path. That is how deeply causality is rooted in our thinking. But that phrasing would be utterly wrong. There is no cause, no effect. No interaction. Only a meaningful coincidence.

Only synchronicity.

ASTROLOGY AS NOTHING BUT COINCIDENCE

People with Scorpio rising are supposedly rather intense. I have Scorpio rising. I have been called rather intense. A modern rationalist would dismiss that observation as "mere coincidence." Time was, I would bristle at such a remark. Now I smile and am inclined to be agreeable.

Coincidence—synchronicity—may well be the single most fundamentally reliable law of the universe. Comparatively, the idea that "for every action, there is an equal but opposite reaction" is proving to be a vague, impressionistic notion of little ultimate scientific worth.

But *Scorpio?* How do the signs of the zodiac get involved in all this? Right in the heart of the notion of synchronicity is the concept of meaning. And signs are meaningful. Arguably, they are the most purely elemental units of significance humanity knows, as basic in their own way as the manner in which our brains process sound and light.

Jung spoke of "archetypes" and considered that they supplied the "glue" of meaning which bound the synchronistic principle to the practical world through what he called "a special psychic instance of probability in general." Beneath any synchronistic coincidence, in other words, one could expect to find one of these primary mythic images.

Thus, the elemental terms of astrology fit squarely into the mechanisms of a synchronistic universe. *In fact, the signs and planets of astrology may be the primordial underlying structures of meaning upon which all synchronistic events hang.* Certainly, they are more basic than the classic Jungian archetypes, which are, to a significant extent, culturally specific.

Jung and Pauli together postulated a quaternity of principles. Energy was set against Space/Time. And Synchronicity was set against Causality. ("Energy" here must be understood in the post-Einsteinian sense, as including matter.) In other words, in the first principle we have all the stuff in the universe and all the juice to move it around. The second principle, Space/Time, supplies an arena in which events can happen.

And why does anything happen? Either of two reasons: something causes the event, or meaning coincides with it.

No common sense? Think of photons. Or your own life.

In the previous chapter, we took pains to demonstrate that there may well be a perfectly rational, causal explanation for the fact that astrology works. In this chapter, we have demonstrated that such an explanation is quite unnecessary.

Which approach is more valid? Does the cosmos contain a force we could call astrological "energy?" Are planetary effects conveyed to us through some physical mechanism?

Or can we explain it all in synchronistic terms?

At this point, I think that any definitive answer is premature. Certainly, the success of horary astrology cannot be explained through any causal model; that's pure synchronicity. But birthchart astrology could be viewed either way. Jung suggests that events occur for either of two reasons. At this point, I'm inclined to imagine that astrology is broad enough to operate through both mechanisms.

13

MIND

The man in the leather jerkin squints, his right hand held wide from his hip, menacing me with his knife. His eyes are cold, hateful, and concentrated. I stare back at him in the same posture, my fingers clutching my own knife, meeting his gaze. We circle each other like two cats on the edge of exploding into a blur of claws and teeth.

A black-haired woman stands nearby, floating between horror and fascination. Whoever survives this knife fight will claim her; that's understood.

His eyes shift, telegraphing his fatal intention. Time slows; suddenly, I have all eternity. I swing my knife fast through a waist-high horizontal arc, ripping the sharp blade through his intestines.

He looks at me, blankly, uncomprehendingly. His knife drops, as a gush of blood pours from the gash below his belly. Without compassion, I back off. I wait for him to fall, to die.

He does.

And I wake up, shaken and covered in sweat. I'm far too nice a fellow to have had a dream like that one.

It's six o'clock in the morning. I lie alone on the bed, getting my bearings. The woman in the dream—I know her. And the man, my enemy … I suspect I know him too.

Six o'clock in the morning. She's five hundred miles away, but it's a workday. I know her schedule. She's awake and getting ready to head for her office in New York City. Impulsively, I phone her. She answers groggily.

I say, "Were you asleep?"

"I must've fallen ba …" Before I can say another word, she says, "My God, Steven, I just had the most horrible dream. I dreamed I was watching a knife-fight. You killed someone …"

The dream still gives me goose bumps, many long years later.

Two people, many miles apart, dreaming the same dream at the same time, each from his or her individual perspective: what are the odds against such an event? Any "rational" explanation feels thin, improbable and contrived. Something else was going on there, something magical.

Magical. But not necessarily unusual.

Almost everyone with whom I discuss the subject has some kind of personal "paranormal" tale to relate. Prophetic dreams, uncanny intuitions, hunches, "extrasensory perceptions" of every flavor: they abound. Even Sigmund Freud, that arch conservative in so many ways, wrote in an essay published posthumously, "If I had my life to live over again, I should devote myself to psychical research rather than to psychoanalysis."

But psychical research is a tough business, maybe even a contradiction in terms. Researchers in the field of telepathy have produced some impressive statistical results. If you're interested in learning about them, I heartily recommend either of Lyall Watson's two inspiring volumes, *Supernature* or *Beyond Supernature*.

Any immersion in the literature of psychic research will, however, immediately confront the reader with one inescapable impression: the human capacity for mental telepathy is a notoriously elusive bird to snare. Investigating it is a lot like investigating astrology, in other words. It is slippery. The most convincing statistical results in existence could be produced right under your nose and you wouldn't have any notion that history was being made until you ran the numbers through a computer.

Guess whether the card in the envelope is black or white. The odds are even. Guess time after time after time. If you're consistently right 55 percent of the time, that is significant. Or wrong 55 percent of the time, for that matter. Either way, the laws of chance are violated, and there is something occurring that demands an explanation.

But you have to spend a whole lot of time guessing about envelopes before the numbers begin to mean anything.

From a scientific viewpoint, even a relatively open-minded one, it appears that while there is some evidence for the reality of human mental telepathy, it remains ambiguous. This mode of perception, as it performs in the laboratory, is weak, unreliable, and practically useless—again, much the way astrology often emerges when we attempt to study it statistically. Witness the Gauquelins' results, as we described them in Chapters Three and Four: significant, but subtle.

Only when the numbers are big enough does the pattern emerge in a convincing way.

The Rhine Institute, formerly part of Durham, North Carolina's Duke University, was for many years the center of world research into the "paranormal." Under the guidance of Dr. J.B. Rhine, countless rigorous studies were conducted. Many produced exactly the type of results to which I referred above: persuasive, but only in terms of the laws of probability.

Toward the end of the 1930s, Rhine personally controlled a tenth of the entire research budget at Duke, due in large part to public enthusiasm and the donations that came with it. Predictably, this produced a political backlash. Eventually, the Institute was forced out of the university, although it survives privately to this day.

As a wide-eyed college freshman in 1967, I came to nearby Chapel Hill to attend the state university. My skill in interpreting symbols was mistaken for "psychic powers," and through a convoluted series of lucky misunderstandings, I was privileged to become rather deeply involved with the Rhine Institute and its cadre of researchers. I even marshaled my courage and marched awestruck up to Dr. Rhine himself one evening and shook his hand. I felt as though Jehovah had allowed me to buy Him a beer.

As my association with the Institute and its people deepened, I became aware that there were really two lines of research being conducted. One was overt, the other covert. Outwardly, the "numbers game" was still pursued vigorously: I did my own share of card-guessing. As a research specimen, I proved barely interesting enough to be kept alive.

But outside the laboratory, there was another realm. Hypnosis, Ouija boards, communication with spirits— much of what nearly two decades later became known as "New Age" territory—we dabbled in all of it there in Durham in the late 1960s. And we often had our enthusiasm rewarded with astonishing experiences.

Under hypnosis, I once located a hidden ring without leaving my chair. I "saw" it in my mind, knew exactly where it was. But I couldn't find it a second time. Statistically, then, nothing happened: just one more "mere anecdote" to add to the pile.

What we seemed to be realizing, back there on the edges of the Rhine Institute, is that human psychic potential and laboratory conditions are not a natural match. In the words of Lyall Watson, "As a biologist, I find these card-guessing tests somewhat meaningless. They seem to me to lack significance and survival value."

It seems that it is hard to be psychic unless we are either responding to some crisis that requires it—or, less dramatically, unless we are quite busily having fun with it.

In *Beyond Supernature*, Watson recounts a tale that is fairly typical. A student at Cambridge University, James Wilson, began to tremble uncontrollably one evening. He felt ill and became convinced he was dying. After three hours, the disorder abated and he went to bed. The next day, he learned that his brother had died that same night.

And another: a fisherman on a vessel in the mid-Pacific took a very bad fall, breaking his back. He lay below decks undiscovered and in excruciating pain. Before losing consciousness, he registered the time: 9:12. Six hundred miles away, the Samoan wife of the vessel's captain felt "a blow at the back of the head." She fell to the floor, and said, "Something very bad has happened on the boat." The clock said 9:14.

In each of these stories, we find the optimal ingredients for human psychic receptivity: crisis, intensity, strong emotions, and *a compelling need* ... even if it's only the "need to know." The violent dream I recounted at the beginning of this chapter fits the pattern. It's an old story: I was being jilted, and I felt all the dreadful emotions of rage and betrayal that go with that dark territory.

And I needed to know.

Mental telepathy begins to resemble synchronicity, as we explored it in the previous chapter. In the synchronistic universe, events may coincide simply because it would be meaningful for them to coincide. And meaning, of course, is a very human concept, and tends almost always to have emotional content. Undoubtedly, it was "emotionally meaningful" for James Wilson to feel ill at the time he was unknowingly losing his brother—or for the captain's wife to sense a crisis that was so relevant to her distant husband. Or for me to begin to accept a hard truth about a failed relationship.

Are telepathy and synchronicity the same? Is extrasensory perception just one category of the law of meaningful coincidence?

If Carl Jung was correct when he proposed that synchronicity and causality are the two pillars of the cosmos, then it is almost certain that synchronicity lies behind psychic phenomena. Why? The process of elimination, mostly: attempts to make sense of ESP in causal terms are not very compelling. With physical models of astrology, we at least have enormous energies at our disposal: the magnetic fields of mighty planets and their huge electric and gravitational potentials. But with telepathic phenomena, all we have are the feeble bioelectrical energies of the human brain. Even with resonance amplification, it is hard to believe that there was a physical effect linking the brain of that unfortunate fisherman and the Samoan woman six hundred miles away.

Psychic, extrasensory sensitivity, if we accept its existence, points toward other, murkier realities far removed from the mechanical universe defined by the laws of cause and effect. But does it point to synchronicity? Or is the link which sometimes appears between one consciousness and another yet a new and distinct power in this cryptic universe?

Perhaps we don't really need an answer. Already, we know enough to propose a third, and quite separate, model of astrological mechanism.

And if the synchronistic model seemed exotic, this one appears downright subversive.

MIND LINK

Plato envisioned the cosmos as a living being. He spoke, as we saw in Chapter Five, of the "intelligence in the heaven" to which our own intelligences "are akin." The idea seems utterly mad from any conventional viewpoint; we have come to think of life as a property of physical organisms. Even if our perspectives are more theological, embracing notions of souls or angels or guiding spirits, we still tend to frame the physical cosmos as merely the arena in which certain moral or evolutionary dramas are being enacted—not as a living entity in and of itself.

But if we only align ourselves with Plato for a moment, how cleanly and clearly astrology fits into the puzzle! *The Great Mind of the universe and our own little minds are simply in a state of telepathic rapport.* No further explanation is necessary.

A restless, meowing kitten wanders in a cage whose floor is divided into two dozen squares. He is watched for forty minutes. Twice during that time, the kitten relaxes, remains in one square for two minutes, and makes no noise.

A half mile away, a young man also relaxes, enters the alpha brain wave state, then announces he is "going." He is "gone" for two minutes, off to comfort the kitten. He "goes" twice. Each time, the cat is quiet.

That experiment, done at Duke University, seems to have nothing whatsoever to do with astrology. And yet it might. Does the part of the living universe which we call Venus do for all of us what that young man did for the anxious kitten? And does it perhaps accomplish that task in exactly the same way?

Is there, in other words, a sympathy of life for life which extends not only horizontally among Earth's creatures but also vertically between ourselves and the great mind of the galaxies?

We don't know. But once again, in propounding this seemingly "unscientific" notion, we find support for it right on the cutting edge of theoretical physics.

THE HOLOGRAPHIC PARADIGM

Most of us have by now had the eerie pleasure of viewing a hologram. So different from a photograph, a hologram seems to hang there in three-dimensional space before our eyes, like a ghost. From new-wave art galleries to bank charge cards, these images are slowly becoming part of the iconography of our time.

How are holograms made? The theory is not terribly obscure. You'll recall that in the previous chapter we spoke of the "interference pattern" generated when light passed through two adjacent slits. The waves from one slit collided with the waves from the other one. Sometimes they reinforced each other; others times, they canceled each other out. Just visualize two rocks hitting the same still pond ten feet apart. What do the waves do? Obviously, it's a complicated interaction. Reinforcing and canceling are just the extremes; every possibility in between exists also.

With all that in mind, add one more thought. Remember that normally, light contains a wide range of wavelengths. That is why "white" sunlight produces rainbows. But a laser beam is light composed of one single wavelength.

Take two lasers, cross the beams, and you will get a fairly simple interference pattern— simpler at least than anything that is likely to occur in nature. Now reflect one of those laser beams off a skull before it crosses the other beam. Record the resulting interference pattern on a photographic plate.

What you have is a hologram.

Visually, it's just a swirling, meaningless design. But shine light on it, get the angle right, and there's that skull floating in space, straight out of a Stephen King novel.

Now shatter the holographic plate. Break it into a hundred pieces. Pick up one of the fragments, shine a light on it again. What do you see? A stain on what was once the left side of the brain cavity? A jaw?

No: you still see the entire skull.

This is one of the most unsettling properties of holography. *Any fragment contains the whole.*

Switch channels. In 1929, Karl Lashley published his research indicating that brains do not store their memories in particular places inside the skull. Contrary to common sense, removing sections of the cerebrum doesn't remove certain memories and skills while leaving others intact. Your memory is really nothing like a library. Our brains, just like holograms, store their information non-locally; each part contains a microcosm of the whole.

Stanford neuroscientist Karl Pribram was the first to suggest that human memory might in fact be a holographic phenomenon. Interference patterns can exist between all forms of energy that express themselves in waves. And nerve impulses in the brain do exactly that, and they may interact just as laser beams do in making a hologram. Thus, from a physical standpoint, your personality, your memories, your skills—all may be described as interference patterns vibrating inside your head. Your consciousness mathematically decodes them and calls them up as images, ideas, and intentions.

Switch channels again. Physicist David Bohm, formerly an associate of Albert Einstein, describes a simple experiment. A drop of insoluble ink is stirred carefully into a vial of glycerin. Slowly, it is drawn out into a fine, thin line. Then it disappears—until the stirring is reversed, whereupon the drop reappears. While the ink is invisible, it is said to be "folded into" the glycerin.

Similarly, suggests Bohm, behind the universe we see there lies a second universe, "folded into" our own. He calls this second universe the "implicate order," and the visible realm, the "explicate order." Thus, spread evenly throughout the cosmos, "folded into" everything, is another, higher order of reality.

Karl Pribram, the brain scientist, realized that David Bohm, the physicist, was describing *a holographic universe*. Every tiny fragment of the explicate cosmos contains a trace of the whole implicate motif.

The universe really does exist in a grain of sand.

To Bohm, the entire world we experience is an interference pattern. Interacting wavelengths of energy on the implicate level come together to produce all the "hard" phenomena of the cosmos. Marilyn Ferguson, writing in *The Holographic Paradigm*, adds, "And the brain's neural interference patterns, its mathematical processes, may be identical to the primary state of the universe."

Which, translated, is really just a modern restatement of the oldest principle in astrology: as above, so below. Mind and sky, brain and universe, are one.

Ferguson goes on, "In a nutshell, the holographic super-theory says that our brains mathematically construct "hard" reality by interpreting frequencies from a dimension transcending time and space. The brain is a hologram, interpreting a holographic universe."

Thus, at the rim of physics, we are witnessing the emergence of a view of ultimate reality into which the basic astrological idea fits like a bolt in a nut. Consciousness looks like the universe. The brain/mind is a fragment of the holographic cosmos and contains in itself an image of the whole. The structure of one, in both space and time, reflects the structure of the other.

And "implicate" in each is something else, an invisible third leg of the tripod from which both mind and cosmos arise.

IN SUMMARY

Shatter the cosmos. Gather up the fragments. What do they look like?

The human mind.

Which is identical to the cosmos.

And the human mind is alive.

Which tells us something similar about the cosmos.

"If the human soul is anything," wrote Carl Jung, "it must be of unimaginable complexity and diversity ... Its non-spatial universe conceals an untold abundance of images which have accumulated over millions of years of living development and become fixed in the organism."

What images?

Primary, synchronistic units of meaning. "Archetypes," to Jung. The stuff of the implicate order. Not planets and signs, simply. Or thoughts either. But something more basic, something behind both the solar system and our states of awareness, invisibly linking and binding them.

An intelligence in the Heaven.

Jung goes on, "Beside this picture I would like to place the spectacle of the starry heavens at night, for the only equivalent of the universe within is the universe without; and just as I reach this world through the medium of the body, so I reach that world through the medium of the psyche."

Mind and Sky.
Siblings.
Bound together, synchronistically, telepathically,
physically.
Yet not alone.
Behind the Two exists One.
Nameless.
Hidden.
Implicate.
Meaningful.
Alive.
What is it?
Close your eyes; look at the sky.
That.

CONCLUSION

TO PART THE VEIL OF NIGHT

*L*una Moth, my little sloop, is anchored in darkness a few miles from the marina. I am on board, alone. Sleepless, I sit on deck, feeling the hard wind blow across the black water. The damp air is chilly and unwelcoming. A gibbous moon is rising out of the sea-mists. Overhead, I see the pale stars of Cygnus and Lyra, shining dimly against the faded Milky Way.

There's stark beauty in the bay and the sky, but no serenity, at least not for me. I'm raw, tired, and vulnerable.

The water is howling. Across a hundred yards of sand and shallows lies Bogue Inlet, the meeting point of the human world and the shadowy, infinite sea. Deep ocean waves hit the shallow water. They rise and curl, then crash in lurid blasts of white foam on the sand. The din is primordial, ancient. It infects me.

I'm nervous in this frail vessel my father built, so small and undefended in the face of the night and the sea's blind omnipotence. And I've been an incompetent sailor today. I blundered into shallow water and ran aground. I lost a vital bolt over the side. The engine won't start, and the wind's direction prevents me from moving from this exposed lagoon to quieter waters.

The sea, the stars: why do I always return to them?

I climb to the roof of the cabin and gaze seaward, over the low dunes, into the gray-black infinity of the cold North Atlantic. It seems to be breathing, undulating under its blanket of heavy, humid air.

The darkness draws me; I am afraid, yet I long to sail out beyond the breakers, off into the murk and the mystery.

My vessel could not survive the passage; it would be splintered by the demonic pounding of the inlet. I am stuck where I am.

There's a metaphor here.

We are all clumsy creatures sometimes, prone to error and bound to fragile vessels of bone and blood. Beyond us lies an incomprehensible sea, dark and endless, dangerous yet magnetic. To pass from here to there we must navigate a terrible inlet: death—and all those little prefigurements of death which come before growth and change.

Moonlight shines over the breathing water, a trail of light leading out toward the shrouded horizon. I lean on the mast, let my eyes follow the bright path. Another metaphor: the moon casts its beams on the eternal secret. It makes a riddling road across the cold, dark water.

I smile; the moon has teased me, a gentle mockery. I am an astrologer. My life revolves around an impossible task: reading moonbeams, unriddling them. Saying what they mean. Squeezing guidance out of them.

And I can't really do it, yet I can't help but try.

The astrologer's dilemma, just like the poet's, is insurmountable: to find words for the ineffable. To part the veil of night. Yet even our failures seem edifying, as though something in the human spirit longs for the restoration of meaning and purpose to the fabric of the cosmos. To be part of that endless, impossible project is to be fully alive. The alternative is unthinkable.

Long after a birthchart session with me, a psychologist said, "Even if everyone else was saying I was crazy, these archetypal stories you told would affirm me. It was incredibly helpful."

A public school teacher said that astrology had "given (her) much more acceptance of life's natural rhythms."

An executive in the recording industry described his birthchart as an "owner's manual" for his particular human personality, and wondered why so many of us flounder around without one.

A woman who created and now runs a successful travel agency echoed his sentiments. "You've given me a blueprint for understanding my personal dynamics," she said, "and by understanding them, given me courage to act."

Feedback of that nature is extraordinarily satisfying. Yet I know I am only a monkey pointing at moonbeams. It is an act of healing contrition for me to be standing on the deck of my night-bound boat, awed and frightened by the immensity of sky and sea. It is good to be stripped that bare … scared, dumb, and naked under the eternal stars.

An astrologer's office is a cozy place, full of cobras. The symbols are powerful. Knowing them, it is easy to be uncanny, easy to impress people, easy to appear phenomenally insightful. Under safe roofs, under incandescent lights, armed with computers and a formidable library, an astrologer can slip into thinking he or she really understands the moon.

Vanity.

We really know so little. Only a few precious tales, handed down uncountable ages. Images, words, a tradition—the precious, melded recollections of a trillion starry, memorized nights, nights that soared over Egypt and Celtic Europe, over Greece and Mesopotamia, steaming Africa, frozen Tibet, over windblown American plains and fluted Andean heights, nights digested and preserved and handed down the generations in coded symbolism.

I am one inheritor of that legacy. Maybe you are too. If not, you easily can be. Astrology is like music. You can appreciate it the first time you hear it, and yet spend a lifetime cultivating your ear.

A letter came today from a woman prominent in the world of business. I'd prepared a reading of her daughter's chart a year or two ago. A teenager, she had listened casually to the tapes when they arrived, then put them away without comment. Two years later, the young woman came to a crisis in her life, torn between college and a youthful marriage proposal. Her mother wrote, "For whatever reason, she dug out the tapes you had done, dusted them off, and listened to them very carefully ... something snapped in her at that point—for the positive. She is now in school."

Her mother added, "Your work was there when one eighteen-year-old was ready to listen, and I think she knew that she was finally listening to herself."

I receive a lot of letters like that one, although not all of them are so articulate. The older I get, the more each one means to me. Standing in the night wind, feeling *Luna Moth* roll and pitch at anchor under the stars, feeling the brevity and fragility of my existence, such letters mean everything.

Sleep finally calls. I check the anchor line, then shift my gaze once more from the crashing, impenetrable waters to the icepick stars. I crawl down into the welcoming womb of the cabin, extinguish the glowing oil lamp, and settle into my berth. I wonder, briefly, whether weariness will overcome the buzz of my nerves.

No need to worry. In moments, I am sailing another sea, older by far than the upstart Atlantic, and navigating by stars that have shone since time was a child.

BIBLIOGRAPHY

Baker, R. Robin, *Human Navigation and the Sixth Sense*, Simon and Schuster, New York, 1981.

Bly, Robert, *Sleepers Joining Hands*, (for the essay: *I Came Out of the Mother Naked*), Harper and Row, New York, 1973.

Burnham, Robert. Jr., *Burnham's Celestial Handbook: An Observer's Guide to the Universe Beyond the Solar System*, Vols. 1-3. Dover, New York. 1978.

Boslough, John, *Stephen Hawking's Universe*, William Morrow, New York. 1985.

Close, Frank, Michael Marten, and Christine Sutton, *The Particle Explosion*, Oxford University Press, 1987.

Demos, Raphael (editor), *Plato Selections*, Charles Scribner's Sons, New York, 1927.

Eisler, Riane, *The Chalice and The Blade*, Harper and Row, San Francisco, 1987.

Ferris, Timothy, *Galaxies*, Harrison House, New York, 1987.

Garin, Eugenio, *Astrology in the Renaissance*, Routledge and Kegan Paul, London, 1983.

Gauquelin, Francoise, *Psychology of the Planets*. ACS Publications, San Diego, 1982.

Gauquelin, Michel, *Birthtimes*, translated by Sarah Matthews, Farrar, Straus & Giroux, New York, 1983.

George, Demetra, *Mysteries of the Dark Moon*, Harper Collins, San Francisco, 1992.

Gleadow, Rupert, *The Origin of the Zodiac*, Atheneum, New York, 1969.

Gribbin, John, *The Death of the Sun*, Delacorte, New York, 1980.

Grossinger, Richard, *The Night Sky*, Sierra Club Books, San Francisco. 1981.

Hawking, Stephen, *A Brief History of Time*, Bantam Books, New York, 1988.

Jeans, Sir James, *Science and Music*, Cambridge University Press, 1937.

Jung, Carl Gustav, *Synchronicity*, translated by R.F.C. Hull, Bollingen Series XX, Princeton University Press, 1960.

Krupp. E.C., *Echoes of the Ancient Skies*, Harper and Row, New York, 1983.

Mitchell, Stephen, editor, *The Enlightened Heart*, Harper and Row, New York, 1989.

Noyes, Robert W., *The Sun, Our Star*, Harvard University Press, 1982.

Playfair, Guy L. and Scott Hill, *The Cycles of Heaven*, Avon, New York, 1978.

Raymo, Chet, *The Soul of the Night*, Prentice-Hall, Englewood Cliffs, New Jersey, 1985.

Sagan, Carl, *Cosmos*, Random House, New York, 1980.

Seymour, Percy, *Astrology: The Evidence of Science*, Penguin, London, 1988.

Tester, Jim, *A History of Western Astrology*, Boydell, Woodbridge, Suffolk, 1987.

van der Post, Laurens, *Jung and the Story of Our Time*, Random House, New York, 1975.

Watson, Lyall, *Supemature*, Doubleday, New York, 1973.

___ . *The Dreams of Dragons*, William Morrow, New York, 1987.

--- *BeyondSupemature*, Bantam, New York, 1988.

West, John Anthony and Jan Gerhard Toonder, *The Case For Astrology*, Penguin Books, Baltimore, 1973.

Wilber, Ken, (editor), *The Holographic Paradigm and other Paradoxes*, Shambhala, Boulder and London, 1982.

_ _ _ . *Quantum Questions: Mystical Writings of the World's Great Physicists*, Shambhala, Boston and London, 1984.

Zukav, Gary, *The Dancing Wu Li Masters*, William Morrow, New York, 1979.

ABOUT THE AUTHOR

Steven Forrest is the author of several astrological bestsellers, including *The Inner Sky, The Book of the Moon, The Book of Pluto,* and the new classic *Yesterday's Sky.*

Steven's work has been translated into a dozen languages, most recently Chinese and Italian. He travels worldwide to speak and teach his brand of choice-centered evolutionary astrology – an astrology which integrates free will, grounded humanistic psychology and ancient metaphysics.

Along with his busy private practice, he maintains active astrological apprenticeship programs in California, Australia, North Carolina, and Europe. He is a founding member of the Ethics Committee of the International Society for Astrological Research (ISAR). About Steven's readings, Jungian analyst Robert Johnson says, "I have had several charts done in my lifetime and none of them—but yours—have escaped the astrologer mistaking so much of the chart as a sounding board for his own ego. You have recovered the divine art to its noble status."

See his website www.forrestastrology.com for more details.

LEARN ASTROLOGY WITH STEVEN FORREST

Interested in learning more about Steven's unique approach to astrology? For a listing of lectures and workshops that are available in a variety of audio and video formats, go to: http://www.forrestastrology.com/store.

Better yet, join the many successful students who have completed **Steven's Astrological Apprenticeship Program,** where he teaches both the specific techniques of interpretation and the style of presentation that have made him one of the most successful and influential astrologers in the world. Steven takes great joy in passing on the teachings and strategies that have worked for him over the years through his Apprenticeship Program.

The Apprenticeship Program presents students with a rare opportunity to learn astrology in a supportive environment of like-minded individuals, who together create a feeling of community and connection, leading to bonds that last throughout life. Some come to the program to train professionally, while others come for personal or spiritual enrichment.

Learn more at www.forrestastrology.com